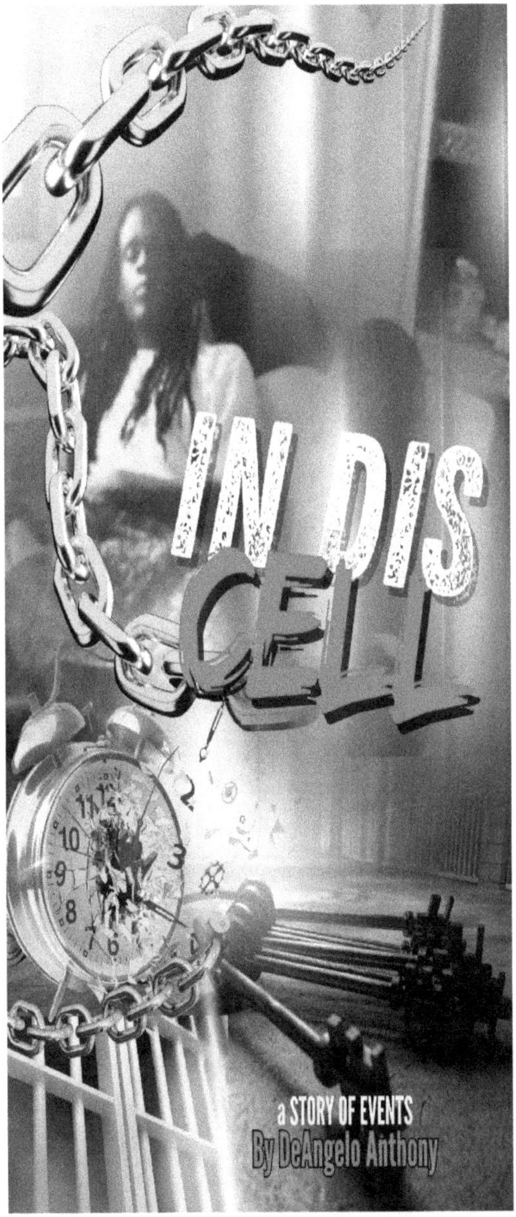
IN DIS
CELL
a STORY OF EVENTS
By DeAngelo Anthony

IN DIS CELL

BY

DEANGELO ANTHONY

Cadmus Publishing
CadmusPublishing.com

IN DIS CELL

Manufactured in the United States of America. Copyright 2025 by Deangelo Anthony   All rights reserved. No part of this book may be reproduced in any form, audio, digital, or in print, except excerpts by reviewers, without written permission from the copyright holder or Cadmus Publishing LLC.

DISCLAIMER:
   The thoughts, opinions, and expressions herein are those of the author and do not reflect those of Cadmus Publishing LLC. Any similarities to actual events or people are purely coincidental. Names and distinguishing characteristics may have been changed to preserve the identities of any individuals. Published by Cadmus Publishing LLC. P. O. Box 8664. Haledon, NJ 07538

Web: Cadmuspublishing.com
Business email: admin@cadmuspublishing.com
ISBN# 978-1-63751-550-1

 Book Catalog Info Categories:
  Memoir

Cadmus Publishing
CadmusPublishing.com

ACKNOWELDGEMENTS

First I would like to thank God for giving me the strength and ability to write my story I would like to thank everyone that supported In Dis Cell video in song I want thank my mother for communicate and encouraging me to push thorough my aspirations and Thank Joi for her designing my book cover

George Kayer and Cadmus publishing for working with me and bringing the book to the people. Thank you. I dedicate this to my children, Myonna and DeAndre and my niece and nephew.

CHAPTER 1 In Dis Cell (Most of My Life)

"The ending is everything. It is the end of the action that determines who gets the glory, the money, the prize."-Robert Greene. One thing for sure I never thought that my life would be interested enough to write my story. I never experienced anything that I deemed worthy of recognition. I remember reading the stories of other great men and women and they all had some huge accomplishments. Their lives were exciting. They were wealthy, had luxurious things and traveled the world. However, me I can't say I've done any of the above... Yet! I don't even know exactly how to write my life story. Where to start at. But I figured the ending is everything. This is not my ending however, I wanted to start with what made me quote on quote 'Famous'. I remember it vividly. I had been in my cell (cell 33 to be exact in housing unit 7) asleep. My cellmate and I had been awakened by several officers in riot gear. They had seemed to thought we were some kind of Cartel Kingpins or something. I had never seen them move in such a manner especially for nothing petty. All I could think about was what my cellmate Treezy told me 'bro when they pull up to our cell deep as fuck, that's when we know we had went viral.' I had laughed because I knew that what had taken place seeing the looks on their faces. The officers cuffed us up one by one and escorted us to A-Wing shower cages. A-Wing is where they housed the segregation

IN DIS CELL DEANGELO ANTHONY

inmates. The sergeant acted like she didn't know what was going on. Treezy had been at Macomb Correctional Facility nearly 5 years and even the officers he had a rapport with refused to tell us what was going on. All I could do was smile. I smiled because I knew that we had just released a music video that had the effect of a nuke and we were about to blow this hell hole to smithereens. LOCKED OFF IN DIS CELL GOT ME CRUSHING DOWN THESE BLUES/FEELING ALL THIS PAIN BARELY CAN TAKE OFF MY SHOES/WORKING ON MY HEART YOU CAN TELL THAT IT BEEN BRUISED/I DONE GAVE MY LOVE AND LOYALTY AND BEEN MISUSED/I had unconsciously began to sing the lyrics to my song In Dis Cell. I melted down the dirty shower walls without care. I had still been in handcuffs and there I was singing like I didn't mind my conditions. Squatting down I closed my eyes listening to my thoughts running wild in my mind. WHATS NEXT? DID WE REALLY GO VIRAL? IF SO WAS IT WORTH WHAT I WILL HAVE TO ENDURE? Treezy being in the same position in the cage next to me chuckled to himself. He said, "Aye ALO. We did that! "We both felt like we had accomplished our mission. We had so many conversations where we plotted and planned to the point we barely spoke about what was really going on. I sat in silence while Treezy yelled to other inmates that we knew playing ignorant, "I don't know why they got us bro!" He acted as if we didn't just get caught with being in possession of two cellphones. The officers were so mad at us for exposing them to the media, they made us stay in the shower cages from 12:30am to 7am that morning.

IN DIS CELL DEANGELO ANTHONY

One of the officers who we had been cool with decided that they strung us out long enough, and he got us moved to our temp seg cells. I walked into the empty cell that had been apparently occupied prior to me being housed there. Guys were calling my name from other cells. I just laid on the bare mate in awe. I thought about how I hoped things would play out. I hadn't seen nor heard what the results actually were at that time, but I thought big since day one. I wanted to get not just my music out to the people but I wanted to show the inhumane treatment we are subjected to here in the MDOC. The world had never been able to see some of the things I displayed and I knew once the fire was set it would be no way for it to be extinguished. One of my homies whom we prepared along the way instantly came to the base. I could almost imagine him leaning over the rail as he said, "Blood y'all all over the news!!" Other fellow inmates praised us for fighting not simply for us, but for them as well. We were in a Residential Treatment Program which is a mental health unit for the MDOC. The caliber prisoners there had been diagnosed with some form of major mental disorder that prohibited them to be housed amongst regular inmates. I suffer from Major depression which is a chronic state that I had developed in my childhood. I'll touch on that once I'm done with what I was explaining. But we were hero's in the eyes of our peers because we could've been like some of the other inmates that had the opportunity to obtain a cellphone device. We chose to capture events that would make a difference. I remember saying to myself, I COULD'VE USED THIS OPPORTUNITY TO GO LIVE TALKING ABOUT IGNORANT

IN DIS CELL DEANGELO ANTHONY

PRISON SHIT. I COULD HAVE SHOWED US BRANDISHING KNIVES, DRUGS ETC. HOWEVER, I THINK I MADE A DIFFERENCE. Oblivious to the fact that we were on every major media outlet as a trending topic, I hadn't seen any of it. All I had as a means of knowing what was what, was every time an officer came down on our rock to do their rounds they'd tell me how many views we were getting. It's like the views climbed by the thousands every day. We would hear 50k, 80k, I even had one of the officers tell me we 'broke the internet'. I was like "broke the internet?" He said "yeah, y'all all over social media and in the Washington Post, New York Post. I see it did like ten million views! "I couldn't believe my ears. It was like some movie type shit. I thought about movies like GET RICH OR DIE TRYING. Or like HUSTLE & FLOW. In fact one of the officers told me when they sent me to maximum security that that's how it would be for me. I felt like some celebrity. I remember being chained up on the hour rec yard we were entitled to and I called home. My mother was like "Deangelo your face is everywhere-

    -I heard they were trying to kill y'all?" My mother sounded so worried. I'm like man I can't reveal what's really going on. I didn't want to have her stressing over things. I always been the child that seemed to always be in the thick of things. But my mother was a team player. She had been rocking with me since juvenile. To be honest, she was the person that forwarded the video to the media on my behalf. My Mama don't play about her children and we had already done something similar to this once before that I'd touch on, but we had built that revolutionary mentality where we found power in the media. So she was telling me about what was going on. She began to lighten up once she heard no worries in my voice. I wasn't worried at all. I just knew that I had done something nobody had ever done. Here it was I was in prison hence 13 yrs, and 11 months and I managed to record a real structured music video all in one prison cell! It was an amazing experience because I had experience as an artist in rap videos when I was in the free world, however, who would have ever thought those skills would come in handy 13 yrs later? I mastered minded the whole video set up. The funny thing about this though, is I had never owned an iPhone. I had never used one before. In fact when I was free I think we were still using Nokia's. We didn't even have touch screens. But I Mastered the technology overnight. I knew everything there was to know about using these devices. I only had one question for my mother after we caught up on this event, AM I FAMOUS? My mother had paused and replied, "Yes! People know your name now like Big Meech." I'm like be for real. I'd never amount to that man. Big Meech is one of my idols. I looked up to his leadership and how he was such a great brother to his homies and a pillar in his community. Despite what he had done in his past, same as me he had strived to make a difference. Now you telling me my mother who is living way on the west coast said people know of me like that? Wow, that was all I could think of. When I had got back to the cell I had a new mentality. The new mentality was prosperous and thankful. I knew it had to be destiny because the universe had lined up so perfectly because the events that led up to this as well as, the events that had taken place after this, it was mathematically designed. It was so scary to realize that my card had been pulled. My calling was at the door and I had just answered the call whether I was ready or not. Recently I was watching one of my favorite preachers/motivational speaker's Bishop T.D Jakes and he had spoken about how David had not known his destiny; however he showed up at the right and exact time. He had went to deliver lunch to his fellow brothers and just so happened to be met with slaying Goliath. This is my Goliath! So the day came around where I was to be heard on the misconduct. I knew I'd beat the misconduct because on September 10th, 2022 I had already been caught with the phone. Oh, they were so pissed, I remember I was on the phone with my brother Jeremi. He had finally seen the video while he was visiting his family in Africa. I was so geek to show him the video because in the song I mentioned him in the song saying that he was praying for me and trying his best to get me to practice Christianity. He had been preaching to a group of African children. My mother told me how he had been seen on Facebook doing exactly what I praised him for in my song. It was amazing to see how things played out. We spoke for a while until Treezy jumped off the bunk and approached the cell door. By this time they had moved all RTP prisoners to 5 blocks while they worked on the cell doors due to them not being about to keep them locked. So Treezy get to cursing the officer out who seemed to had been doing a round however, little did we know they were there to raid our cell. I listened in and realized what was going on and I instantly turned the device off and put it in my underwear. Had to keep the tightly whites on in case of time like this. The officers could be heard discussing their plan of entry. That time it wasn't like the time they came when the video went viral. This was just two officers so I figured it would be like every other time they searched our cell. Plus, Treezy and I had made a pact whoever get caught with the phone or be in possession of it would have to destroy it if they corner us. That whoever happened to be me. My mother even said, "always DeAngelo." As the officer attempted to cuff me I side stepped him and luckily the other officer took his attention off me giving me time to gauge the situation. I weighed my options and seen that they were going to do everything possible to confiscate the phone. They had been tipped off by another facility due to one of my homies whom had passed away shortly afterwards held a conversation with another one of my homies who had been on Security Threat Group Two status. Beside, all calls are subjected to monitoring and recording. I guess the homies didn't get that memo. Anyway, I saw it being no other way and I didn't want them to see anything we had on that phone. Thus, I pulled the phone from my pants and smashed it into pieces. The phone bounced off the walls on the base galley. The officer who the administration used as their drug dog was shocked. He came for the phone he just didn't expect my reaction to be so swift and unapologetic. I had been placed in the same seg showers I told you about previously. However, this time after they shook my area of control down they released me with a bondable ticket. Meaning I was back out from seg walking to the chow hall as if nothing just happened. I had been later given 25 days Loss of privileges and that was that. November 20, 2022 had a different outcome. The hearings officer heard my side of the story. I had plead not guilty due to the fact I had already been charged and heard on that same misconduct twice for the same phone. So the hearings officer dismissed the misconduct December 1, 2022. After the misconduct was dismissed I felt like I had beaten them at their own game. I remember planning on how I would celebrate once they release me back out to General Population. What I was going to Cook up, who I was going to call first. That was far from what they had in store for me. The inspector and the Assistant Warden along with the Rum had all came to hold a classification hearing. I listened to them as they tried to interrogate me. It was so funny because these inspectors watched too much First 48 episodes. I played dumb as a box of rocks. They had showed me my Instagram and the YouTube page. I still said that ain't me. It was quite amusing to be frank. The rum had said a sarcastic remark, "hey may be Kanye West will sign you? You did like millions of views." He referred due to the White Lives Matter situation Kanye had been dealing with in the media. Another way to be rhetorical. After they tried to run game on me they had admitted that they messed up regards to me because they missed the fact I had already been charged 60 days prior to this November misconduct. They didn't know what to do with me. Per policy I was to be released back to the yard but after what I did exposing their officers for doing the foulest of the foulest of things, I knew I was heading to the upper room. In my video IN DIS CELL I had captured officers dragging one of my friends body through sewage water after he attempted to get help from one of the officers who had been antagonizing him. This officer had taunted him to the brink of committing suicide to get away from the way he was being treated. I had also captured a full-scale riot/lockdown. There was a hit placed on the Rum who I had mentioned above that made the Kanye remark. He had been such an asshole that someone allegedly placed a hit on him. The hitman attempted to do the job so he says, however it came out he went into the office and gave the Rum the knife and told on some guys who I had been associated with. Then during all of this the inmates popped their sprinkler heads releasing sewage water flooding the halls and cells. The officers even fed us in unsanitary environments. It was a mess and this was what they had displayed on every Major News Station and Major Free Press Nationwide. In fact globally. Awaiting their verdict I was so anxious in my cell. The officers I knew would come and tell me how they had the Media Outlets parked outside demanding to interview us. What made me really understand the magnitude of this was one of the female officers who later had resigned due to her colleagues harassing her had told me her two little daughters at a middle school asked her did she know the rappers at the prison. She bragged about being an officer with direct access to us in the unit she worked in. I couldn't believe this white lady two little girls seen this video. I even had inmates that had come over to watch the prisoners on 'suicide watch' ask me for my autograph. Like I signed my first autograph to an inmate there at Macomb with me. I thought, WOW I GUESS I AM FAMOUS. Later that victorious night, the Acting Warden had made his round and informed me that I was riding out to another facility. Honestly I was optimistic about being transferred to another RTP facility. That wasn't the case. I see the ICF initials on my paperwork and knew I was being sent back to maximum security at Ionia Correctional Facility. They smuggled me into Ionia Max at nearly 1am December 2, 2022. I remember peering out the window the entire time admiring the night skies. I imagined being free and thought about how much I missed traveling those late nights on the highways. It's like we brought all the stars out. They shined and twinkled almost as a sign saying, ITS GOING TO BE OKAY. Treezy and I did our little building anticipating being separated. I'm like "you you got to be strong. Think retaliation and harassment at its highest form. Just stay focused and mentally prepared to override the oppression ahead." The look on his face told me he would be okay and that no matter what my dog will continue to scratch and stand for what we believed in. Being at Ionia Max earlier in my bid, I had felt the same exact feeling I had the first time going to maximum security. It wasn't fear of the inmates or the yard but I could hear my father's voice giving me his account of being an inmate at Ionia Max when it was a level 6. "Boy them white people there is crazy! They tried to kill me because I had filed a law suit on them back in the day...," he always told me this stories every chance he got. My mind was set though. I refused to even be treated anywhere near the way they did my father. I felt protected because I knew what I had and I knew that the administration is smarter than that. I just assumed they would stay out of my way and I would do the same with them. When I exited the transport van, two officers met me with huge smiles. Confused I just went along with their energy. "Hey we saw that video," one of them said. "It was funny." I lightly chuckled HA HA HA, I'm sure they were laughing with the same POV as I. I was laughing at them not with them. Likewise. I walked thru the thresholds as the door buzzed us in. There was another officer that helped with the escort. He was a stereotypical officer. "When you're being escorted here at IMAX don't look to the side or in any direction other than forward, otherwise we will take you to the ground as if you were attempting to spit on us!" He made it clear that I wasn't welcomed in the sense you'd think by the way they all spoke about the video. They took me to seg for the weekend. I slept...

"You cannot have growth without disruption"- Bishop T.D Jakes. I was born a stillborn March 17, 1989 in the city of Detroit, Michigan at Grace Hospital. My mother Dewanda Jones had delivered me and discovered that I had bacteria in my system. My father had been in prison a month or so into my mother's pregnancy. As bad as it seems coming into this world dead, it wasn't a coincidence that I was born at Grace Hospital. Someone had grace for me because they rushed me off to save my life. "God had mercy on my soul," as my grandmother would say. My mother said that she would come up to the hospital to visit me and I would be in this baby crib at the hospital that reminded her of a cage or a prison cell because it had steel bars. I can't lie it moved me because we recently had a conversation where she told me about this. When I came home we lived on the East side of Detroit in the Martin Luther King Homes. The King homes was the unadulterated definition of what a project was. That complex was and still is to this day one of the most dangerous neighborhoods in the city of Detroit. It was infested with drugs, crime and some very violent individuals. To me as a child, that was probably one of the best environments I can remember that I loved living in. Around this time my mother had only me and my older brother David Jr. She raised us in a single parent household funded by government assistance. My mother was still young and in her party mode with her partner in crime, my aunty Kim. My aunty Kim was my Uncle Michael children's mother. He was the first male figure ever in my life that I can think back on. His daughters would babysit me and my brother while our mother's went clubbing. My cousin Elisha was the youngest of the three daughters my aunty Kim had. I was raised by nothing but strong women. My cousin Elisha showed me how to be responsible. She was the one that made sure we did all the chores. Looking back I think once our mothers left she had so many chores she used us as minions to do her cleaning. It was funny because she was so young and had been a natural nurturer. I had a best friend named Bae Bae. Bae Bae's mother became my mother and aunties party buddy as well. So they would leave me and Bae Bae with Elisha and my cousins Jennifer, and Keisha. Bae Bae and I would play as children did. Bae Bae was bad as hell. We both would influence one another to be devious kids.

IN DIS CELL DEANGELO ANTHONY

We would run around the projects bullying the other kids our age. It was to the point me and Bae Bae could only manage to get along with each other. We even would fight each other. He always had long nails and would scratch my face up when we fought. I remember my cousin Jennifer had told us that girls scratch and pull hair. She showed us how to throw hands. She was a beast growing up. She was light skinned and back then it was like they had it hard in school. She fought girls at her school and in the neighborhood all the time. She was the one that sort of implemented that aggression I needed to defend and survive even to this day. She taught me to stand up for myself and others. The first time I ever met a real street guy or somebody who fits the category as a Gangsta, was my mother's boyfriend Keith. Keith was my first introduction to guns etc. I had to be no more than five years old. I remember one day he had done something in the projects and the police had been searching for him. He had run to my mother's apartment to hide. I remember hearing sirens and seeing all the flashing lights dancing about the small bedroom. Keith had a .38 Special that had grey duct tape wrapped around the handle. How I remember that you'd think I stole a scene from 'Menace To Society', but when I was little he let me hold that same revolver and from that day I knew I wanted to be a Gangsta or thug. I feel in love with guns and being the bad child. Keith never got caught that particular night he hid in the closet until the police gave up their search. Sadly though he had killed a few guys and his lifestyle caught up with him and he ended up being killed. Meeting Keith was the highlight of my journey to Prison. My mother hadn't realized that

IN DIS CELL DEANGELO ANTHONY

I would have been deeply influenced by one of her boyfriends in the past. I would mimic the street guys around the projects. They carried pagers and big ass cellphones; I went to the local liquor stores and bought the see thru pagers and phones that had been filled with bubblegum. They carried revolvers I went and grabbed cap guns that looked exactly like the real deal. I even went as far as saving brown dollar food stamps like I had a bankroll of cash. It was funny because Bae Bae and I had actually thought we were like the older guys in the projects. Before I move forward with the story I got to share this event that I can say was like my first gang like activity. Bae Bae mother had held his birthday party at a place for kids called Major-Magics. It was like a spinoff of Chucky cheese. They had the big rats and all. I remember Bae Bae and I had seen this huge Masqat and I just remember us attacking this poor guy who was there to entertain the kids. We was on him like he had stolen something. Our mother's couldn't do nothing but shake their heads like these lil boys something else. My mother ended up meeting a new boyfriend by the name of Rick. We had moved out the King Homes and had moved back into my childhood house on Six Mile and Strasbourg that my aunty Nancy lived at. I don't really remember too much about living in that house at that time. I just remember it was this little yellow toy car that was passed down from my brother David to me. It had only three wheels on it. We stayed at this house with my aunty who was one of my favorite aunts. She showed me how to tap into my creative side. She made music, wrote books, made clothes etc. The look on his face told me he would be okay and that no matter what, my dog will continue to scratch and stand for what we believed in. Being at Ionia Max earlier in my bid, I had felt the same exact feeling I had the first time going to maximum security. It wasn't fear of the inmates or the yard, but I could hear my father's voice giving me a recount of being an inmate at Ionia Max when it was a level 6. "Boy them white people there is crazy! They tried to kill me because I had filed a lawsuit on them back in the day...," he always told me this story every chance he got. My mind was set though. I refused to ever be treated anywhere near the way they did my father.

    I felt protected because I knew what I had and I knew that the administration is smarter than that. I just assumed they would stay out of my way and I would do the same with them. When I exited the transport van, two officers met me with huge smiles. Confused, I just went along with their energy. "Hey, we seen that video," one of them said. "It was funny." I lightly chuckled—HA HA HA—I'm sure they weren't laughing with the same POV as I. I was laughing at them, not with them. Likewise.

    I walked through the thresholds as the door buzzed us in. There was another officer that helped with the escort. He was a stereotypical officer. "When you're being escorted here at IMax, don't look to the side or in any direction other than forward, otherwise we will take you to the ground as if you were attempting to spit on us!" He made it clear that I wasn't welcomed in the sense you'd think by the way they all spoke about the video. They took me to seg for the weekend. I slept...

CHAPTER 2 In Dis Cell (Most of my life)

"You cannot have growth without disruption" – Bishop T.D. Jakes.

I was born a stillborn March 17, 1989, in the city of Detroit, Michigan at Grace Hospital. My mother Dewanda had delivered me and discovered that I had bacteria in my system. My father had been in prison a month or so into my mother's pregnancy. As bad as it seems coming into the world dead, it wasn't a coincidence that I was born at Grace Hospital. Someone had grace for me because they rushed me off to save my life. "God had mercy on my soul," as my grandmother would say.

My mother said that she would come up to the hospital to visit me and I would be in this baby crib at the hospital that reminded her of a cage or a prison cell because it had steel bars. I can't lie; it moved me because we recently had a conversation where she told me about this.

When I came home we lived on the East Side of Detroit in the Martin Luther King Homes. The King Homes was the unadulterated definition of what a project was. That complex was, and still is to this day, one of the most dangerous neighborhoods in the city of Detroit. It was infested with drugs, crime, and some very violent individuals. To me as a child, that was probably one of the best environments I can remember that I loved living in.

Around this time my mother had only me and my older brother David Jr. She raised us in a single-parent household funded by government assistance. My mother was still young and in her party mode with her partner in crime, my aunty Kim. My aunty Kim was my Uncle

Michael's children's mother. He was the first male figure ever in my life that I can think back on. His daughters would babysit me and my brother while our mothers went clubbing.

My cousin Elisha was the youngest of the three daughters my aunty Kim had. I was raised by nothing but strong women. My cousin Elisha showed me how to be responsible. She was the one that made sure we did all the chores. Looking back, I think once our mothers left, she had so many chores she used us as minions to do her cleaning. It was funny because she was so young and had been a natural nurturer.

I had a best friend named Bae Bae. Bae Bae's mother became my mother and aunties' party buddy as well. So they would leave me and Bae Bae with Elisha, my cousin Jennifer, and Keisha. Bae Bae and I would play as children did. Bae Bae was bad as hell. We both would influence one another to be devious kids. We would run around the projects bullying the other kids our age. It was to the point me and Bae Bae could only manage to get along with each other. We even would fight each other. He always had long nails and would scratch my face up when we fought.

I remember my cousin Jennifer had told us that girls scratch and pull hair. She showed us how to throw hands. She was a beast growing up. She was light-skinned and back then it was like they had it hard in school. She fought girls at her school and in the neighborhood all the time. She was the one that sort of implemented that aggression I needed to defend and survive even to this day. She taught me to stand up for myself and others.

IN DIS CELL DEANGELO ANTHONY

The first time I ever met a real street guy or somebody who fits the category as a Gangsta was my mother's boyfriend Keith. Keith was my first introduction to guns etc. I had to be no more than five years old. I remember one day he had done something in the projects and the police had been searching for him. He had run to my mother's apartment to hide. I remember hearing sirens and seeing all the flashing lights dancing about the small bedroom. Keith had a .38 Special that had grey duct tape wrapped around the handle. How I remember that, you'd think I stole a scene from *Menace II Society*, but when I was little he let me hold that same revolver and from that day I knew I wanted to be a Gangsta or thug. I fell in love with guns and being the bad child. Keith never got caught that particular night—he hid in the closet until the police gave up their search. Sadly though, he had killed a few guys and his lifestyle caught up with him and he ended up being killed. Live by the gun, die by the gun.

My aunty Nancy is they reason I developed such an imagination that I would cultivate over the course of my life. This imagination is also what enabled me to navigate my imprisonment. We stayed with my aunty and my grandmother had come to visit us in Detroit. My grandmother Arizona Jenkins was an amazing black woman from the south. She was an Apostolic Preacher and had her own congregation called Greater Rose of Sharing. My grandmother was one of the first female pastors and preachers that traveled all over the nation preaching the word. She had lived in Memphis, Tennessee and anywhere my grandmother went it was like the entire family would follow. My mother being the baby out her 14 siblings, she decided that we would have a better life in Memphis. We had moved to East Memphis. East Memphis around that time was a very good suburban neighborhood. Her house was this big white house. They drove Lincoln Town Cars and made sure we had the best of everything. When we moved into her house my mother had then had her third child. My sister Meon was adorable. I was finally the big brother and I always would treat her like I wanted to be treated. For some reason growing up my brother never liked me as far as it looked. I don't remember all the fights people said we had but I heard he kicked me down flights of stairs all kinds of things. But I will touch more on me and my sisters bond. I think this was around the time I started truly understanding things. In church you was indoctrinated young about the things that could led you to living a heavenly lifestyle, and you had the part where you were warned about all the sins you commit that ultimately on the Day of Judgement you'd go to hell for. I was told that at the age of like 12 yrs old you are accountable for your own actions and everything previously done is on your parents. So I gained most of my morality from the apostolic faith base. My grandmother made sure I was in Sunday school, front row and I had better paid close attention. The music is what really made me comfortable. It was like those songs we sung touched my soul. I had even joined the choir. It wasn't like I had a choice honestly. My grandmother had the entire family at Church and it was like a family heritage. The Church congregation was the first organized function that I was introduced to. My grandmother was like everybody big homie. She was a magnificent woman. Everybody in the

IN DIS CELL DEANGELO ANTHONY

Church loved her. Real talk I think she was loved and admired by all. People would come to my grandmother's house for advice and prayer. She had dedicated people that would come to her house and help her around the crib. My grandfather was like everybody else's grandfather. He was the one that made sure things were working like a well-oiled machine. He would fix everything in the church, around the house he would also fix the cars man he was multi-talented. Them together was the dynamic dual. They parented the entire neighborhood and some. Before I move too far ahead I got to tell you about James Jenkins. My grandfather was of a rare breed. He was from down south. I never knew much about his side of the family but I know when my mother was younger my grandfather had been hit in the head with a rifle during one of the wars America fought. He earned a purple heart. Back in the day he had raised my mother and her siblings on the Westside of Detroit. My aunty Earnestine had a boyfriend who was in the dope game. They say my grandfather came home one day and the guy was in his house and he told the guy, "boy! Didn't I tell you I don't want you around here?" My grandfather said something it was law. So I guess the guy went and said, "C'mon na mister Jenkins?" Before he knew it my grandfather had blown the man brains out in front of the whole family. He ended up beating the murder due to pleading insanity. It's crazy how many people told me this story. My family has strong ties on Schoolcraft and one of the biggest gangsta from that area had once told me this story in awe. It was like that event even influenced him during his days of playing the streets. But back to Memphis. I mentioned this about my grandfather because I wanted you to see the mentality that I had adopted. I had some strong people raising me and they had dealt with their life struggles but they had been big time drug dealers, bank robbers etc. Drugs even played a huge role in my family. As a child I'm downloading all these attributes into my head which was shaping my mentality. Music had somehow made its way into my life. It was first through the church and later my cousin Deon had introduced me to rap music. Tupac was his favorite rapper and I would be getting my hair cut listening to Pac with him. I knew all the lyrics and the influence Pac had over the black community I became a product of it. I even remember when he had died I cried. It's funny how it played out. My mother had a Tilblue Honda Civic with some little rims. All my cousins had been out in the street, everybody got they radio tuned in to the station that played all Tupac music in commemoration to the fallen rapper. I see everybody else huddled up crying and all I thought he was my uncle or something. So here it was my lil black ass crying in the front driver seat of my mother's car like I knew Pac. It was funny. But around that time I had gotten more curious. They even started calling me Curious George the little monkey. I use to get so mad about that. They would say because I had little ears and they stuck out I looked like a little monkey. That had become one of the things I hated most. I had started school in Memphis. I went to Balmoral Elementary school. I had been suspended on my first day of school for pulling the fire alarm. What's really funny is my daughter did the exact same thing!

IN DIS CELL DEANGELO ANTHONY

East Memphis had been predominantly a white neighborhood in the 90's. My best friend named was White David. We called him White David because my brother David lived with us too and we use to get them mixed up. White David and his family was the first white family that I had ever met. It also was the first time I had been exposed to racism. He had the stereotypical white family. His father name was Guy. His mother acted nice but was racist as hell. His Dog was even racist but Guy was that guy. He was the one I guess suffered from White guilt because he made sure my grandmother had all the fruit and kept her yard clean etc. The wife was a low key freak she actually liked black people I guess the way I use to catch my cousin Deon sneaking out their house. He would be sneaking out the house from doing whatever with the wife and me and my cousin Brittany would be sneaking out the garage from stealing all the ice cream and popsicles. But White David and I would play all the time. I was always the robber and he was the cop. Back then the police would ride around the neighborhood and if you stopped them as a child they would give you a toy police badge. I had got one before but I always played a better bad guy or Villain. I was the robber or an Indian during Cow Boys and Indian's. I would go watch all the kids' movies at White Davids house. Toy Story, Lion King you name it. He had all the best toys and things. I really loved being at his house. But I remember they had a daughter. She was a little older than me and I used to like her. She was my first white girl crush. I can reflect back on the time I had liked her so much I went to Balmoral Elementary School and had found my first white girlfriend. We had got caught during naptime dry-humping. I would get suspended so much in Elementary school to the point it was like I didn't even go to school. To give you a better look at the way my environment sort of shaped my mentality, I remember one day I had been snooping around my mother's room. My stepfather Rick had a loaded gun hid somewhere I can't remember exactly where, but I had found this gun. It was in a leather holster. I had been posing with this gun in the mirror as if I was this gangsta. I had even gone as far as carrying the gun around the house. My cousin Carman had been downstairs watching her stories. Carman was in a wheelchair and a lot of the times she would be the one watching the kids if my grandmother was sleep or something. My grandmother rarely left us alone. But I had this big gun and I remember Carman sitting there watching her shows. I had snuck up behind her and pointed the gun to the back of her head and said, "break yo'self-fool!" So she obviously coulee feel the cold steel on the back of her head and she instantly got scared and started yelling at me. She told on me so fast and I really didn't even realize that the gun was real and it was loaded. Man my mother, my grandmother, my stepfather and my grandfather beat me with belts, switches. Oh my grandfather whooping was the worst. He would make us go pick out twigs and he would braid them. It's ironic because my father's dad uses to do the same thing. I'll touch on Mister A very soon. But yeah they beat my ass! By the time I had reached the second grade my mother had moved to Marina Cove apartment complex. I had a bunk bed. Me and my brother shared the room. My stepfather had married my mother and this was the moment they decided to create a household. Rick was a real nigga whether I felt that way as a child. He did a lot of thing that I later leaned on while doing time. I mean he put me thru some shit but it was to make me strong because he knew I was going to be incarcerated when I had gotten old enough. So Rick would be abusive mentally, physically and emotionally. He wasn't so much beating my mother, but he would beat her children. My brother David was smart though; he had caught on at an early age and went to live with my cousins. But back then every time I'd get suspended or something Rick would do things like make us sleep on the balcony during the winter time. Or he would make us work out or just flat out whoop us. I was a straight A student in school. It wasn't the fact I wasn't able to pass, it was the fact I was just so problematic the schools couldn't handle me. I use to think most of my mother fights with my stepfather was behind my actions because I was so bad. Onetime my mother and my stepfather had got into a physical altercation. He had apparently put his hands on my mother. My aunty Dorothy had been in town and she was for no games. Aunt Dottie was a real street nigga. She did it all. I'll touch more on aunty Dorothy in later in my life story because she played a huge role as well. But I remember she had come over with a machine gun. I have never seen Rick so scared. Even after seeing that I watched my mother go back to him every time. I even seen them fight and someone would call the police on Rick. The police would show up and my mother would deny things ever happened and if the police didn't believe he she would fight with the police and both her and Rick would be locked up. Yeah, they had one of them type relationships. But here's where I would say Rick was a real nigga outside the bullshit he did, but he'd always lose that real nigga moment. One day we had made a pact that if I bring back good grades he would get me some new shoes. So one day he had brought me a pair of Grant Hills. They were the black and green ones. I had just got them and I remember soon as Rick would get mad or fall out with my mother he'd do some hoe shit. So this nigga went and took the Grant Hills he had just brought me and threw them in the pond that encircled the complex. I cried so hard because I had thought we were just getting that stepfather/stepson bond. Rick seen how it affected me and decided to admit....

Meeting Keith was the highlight of my journey to prison. My mother hadn't realized that I would have been deeply influenced by one of her boyfriends in the past. I would mimic the street guys around the projects. They carried pagers and big cellphones; I went to the local liquor stores and bought the see-through pagers and phones that had been filled with bubblegum. They carried revolvers; I went and grabbed cap guns that looked exactly like the real deal. I even went as far as saving brown food stamps like I had a bankroll of cash. It was funny because Bae Bae and I had actually thought we were like the older guys in the projects.

Before I move forward with the story, I got to share this event that I can say was like my first gang-like activity. Bae Bae's mother had held his birthday party at a place for kids called Major-Magics. It was like a spin-off of Chuck E. Cheese. They had the big rats and all. I remember Bae Bae and I had seen this huge mascot and I just remember us attacking this poor guy who was there to entertain the kids. We was on him like he had stolen something. Our mothers couldn't do nothing but shake their heads like, "These lil boys something else."

My mother ended up meeting a new boyfriend by the name of Rick. We had moved out of the King Homes and had moved back into my childhood house on Six Mile and Strasbourg that my aunty Nancy lived at. I don't really remember too much about living in that house at that time. I just remember it was this little yellow toy car that was passed down from my brother David to me. It had only three wheels on it. We stayed at this house with my aunty who was one of my favorite aunts. She showed me how to tap into my creative side. She made music, wrote books, made clothes, etc.

My aunty Nancy is the reason I developed such an imagination that I would cultivate over the course of my life. This imagination is also what enabled me to navigate my imprisonment.

We stayed with my aunty, and my grandmother had come to visit us in Detroit. My grandmother, Arizona Jenkins, was an amazing Black woman from the South. She was an Apostolic preacher and had her own congregation called Greater Rose of Sharon. My grandmother was one of the first female pastors and preachers that traveled all over the nation preaching the word. She had lived in Memphis, Tennessee, and anywhere my grandmother went, it was like the entire family would follow. My mother, being the baby out of her 14 siblings, decided that we would have a better life in Memphis.

We had moved to East Memphis with my grandparents. East Memphis around that time was a very good suburban neighborhood. Their house was this big white house. They drove Lincoln Town Cars and made sure we had the best of everything. When we moved into her house, my mother had then had her third child. My sister Meon was adorable. I was finally the big brother and I always would treat her like I wanted to be treated. For some reason growing up, my brother never liked me as far as it looked. I don't remember all the fights people said we had, but I heard he kicked me down flights of stairs—all kinds of things. But I will touch more on me and my sister's bond.

I think this was around the time I started to truly understand things. In church you were indoctrinated young about the things that could lead you to living a heavenly lifestyle, and you had the part where you were warned about all the sins you commit that ultimately, on the Day of Judgment, you'd go to hell for. I was told that at the age of like 12 years old you are accountable for your own actions and everything previously done is on your parents. So I gained most of my morality from the

Apostolic faith base. My grandmother made sure I was in Sunday School, front row, and I had better paid close attention. The music is what really made me comfortable. It was like them songs we sung touched my soul. I had even joined the choir. It wasn't like I had a choice honestly. My grandmother had the entire family at church and it was like a family heritage.

    The church congregation was the first organized function that I was introduced to. My grandmother was like everybody's big homie. She was a magnificent woman. Everybody in the church loved her. Real talk, I think she was loved and admired by all. People would come to my grandmother's house for advice and prayer. She had dedicated people that would come to her house and help her around the crib.

    My grandfather was like everybody else's grandfather. He was the one that made sure things were working like a well-oiled machine. He would fix everything in the church, around the house, he would also fix the cars—man, he was multi-talented. Them together was the dynamic duo. They parented the entire neighborhood and some.

    Before I move too far ahead, I got to tell you about James Jenkins. My grandfather was of a rare breed. He was from down South. I never knew much about his side of the family but I know when my mother was younger, my grandfather had been hit in the head with a rifle during one of the wars America fought. He earned a Purple Heart. Back in the day, he had raised my mother and her siblings on the Westside of Detroit.

IN DIS CELL DEANGELO ANTHONY

East Memphis had been predominantly a white neighborhood in the 90's. My best friend named was White David. We called him White David because my brother David lived with us too and we use to get them mixed up. White David and his family was the first white family that I had ever met. It also was the first time I had been exposed to racism. He had the stereotypical white family. His father name was Guy. His mother acted nice but was racist as hell. His Dog was even racist but Guy was that guy. He was the one I guess suffered from White guilt because he made sure my grandmother had all the fruit and kept her yard clean etc. The wife was a low key freak she actually liked black people I guess the way I use to catch my cousin Deon sneaking out their house. He would be sneaking out the house from doing whatever with the wife and me and my cousin Brittany would be sneaking out the garage from stealing all the ice cream and popsicles. But White David and I would play all the time. I was always the robber and he was the cop. Back then the police would ride around the neighborhood and if you stopped them as a child they would give you a toy police badge. I had got one before but I always played a better bad guy or Villain. I was the robber or an Indian during Cow Boys and Indian's. I would go watch all the kids movies at White Davids house. Toy Story, Lion King you name it. He had all the best toys and things. I really loved being at his house. But I remember they had a daughter. She was a little older than me and I used to like her. She was my first white girl crush. I can reflect back on the time I had liked her so much I went to Balmoral Elementary School and had found my first white girlfriend. We had got caught during naptime dry-humping. I would get suspended so much in Elementary school to the point it was like I didn't even go to school. To give you a better look at the way my environment sort of shaped my mentality, I remember one day I had been snooping around my mother's room. My stepfather Rick had a loaded gun hid somewhere I can't remember exactly where, but I had found this gun. It was in a leather holster. I had been posing with this gun in the mirror as if I was this gangsta. I had even went as far as carrying the gun around the house. My cousin Carman had been downstairs watching her stories. Carman was in a wheelchair and a lot of the times she would be the one watching the kids if my grandmother was sleep or something. My grandmother rarely left us alone. But I had this big gun and I remember Carman sitting there watching her shows. I had snuck up behind her and pointed the gun to the back of her head and said, "break yo'self-fool!" So she obviously coulee feel the cold steel on the back of her head and she instantly got scared and started yelling at me. She told on me so fast and I really didn't even realize that the gun was real and it was loaded. Man my mother, my grandmother, my stepfather and my grandfather beat me with belts, switches. Oh my grandfather whooping was the worst. He would make us go pick out twigs and he would braid them. It's ironic because my father's dad use to do the same thing. I'll touch on Mister A very soon. But yeah they beat my ass! By the time I had reached the second grade my mother had moved to Marina Cove apartment complex. I had a bunk bed. Me and my brother shared the room. My stepfather had married my mother and this was the moment they decided to create a household. Rick was a real nigga whether I felt that way as a child. He did a lot of thing that I later leaned on while doing time. I mean he put me thru some shit but it was to make me strong because he knew I was going to be incarcerated when I had gotten old enough. So Rick would be abusive mentally, physically and emotionally. He wasn't so much beating my mother, but he would beat her children. My brother David was smart though, he had caught on at an early age and went to live with my cousins. But back then every time I'd get suspended or something Rick would do things like make us sleep on the balcony during the winter time. Or he would make us work out or just flat out whoop us. I was a straight A student in school. It wasn't the fact I wasn't able to pass, it was the fact I was just so problematic the schools couldn't handle me. I use to think most of my mother fights with my stepfather was behind my actions because I was so bad. Onetime my mother and my stepfather had got into a physical altercation. He had apparently put his hands on my mother. My aunty Dorothy had been in town and she was for no games. Aunt Dottie was a real street nigga. She did it all. I'll touch more on aunty Dorothy in later in my life story because she played a huge role as well. But I remember she had come over with a machine gun. I haven't never seen Rick so scared. Even after seeing that I watched my mother go back to him every time. I even seen them fight and someone would call the police on Rick. The police would show up and my mother would deny things ever happened and if the police didn't believe he she would fight with the police and both her and Rick would be locked up.

Yeah, they had one of them type relationships. But here's where I would say Rick was a real nigga outside the bullshit he did, but he'd always lose that real nigga moment. One day we had made a pact that if I bring back good grades he would get me some new shoes. So one day he had brought me a pair of Grant Hills. They were the black and green ones. I had just got them and I remember soon as Rick would get mad or fall out with my mother he'd do some hoe shit. So this nigga went and took the Grant Hills he had just brought me and threw them in the pond that encircled the complex. I cried so hard because I had thought we were just getting that stepfather/stepson bond. Rick seen how it affected me and decided to admit....

But back to Memphis. I mentioned this about my grandfather because I wanted you to see the mentality that I had adopted. I had some strong people raising me and they had dealt with their life struggles but they had been big time drug dealers, bank robbers, Preachers etc. Drugs even played a huge role in my family. As a child I'm downloading all these attributes into my head which was shaping my mentality. Music had somehow made its way into my life. It was first through the church and later my cousin Deon had introduced me to rap music. Tupac was his favorite rapper and I would be getting my hair cut listening to Pac with him. I knew all the lyrics and the influence Pac had over the black community I became a product of it. I even remember when he had died I cried. It's funny how it played out. My mother had a Honda Civic with some little rims. All my cousins had been out in the street, everybody got they radio tuned in to the station that played all Tupac music in commemoration to the fallen rapper. I see everybody else huddled up crying. I thought he was my uncle or something. So here it was my lil black behind crying in the front driver seat of my mother's car like I knew Pac. It was funny. But around that time I had gotten more curious. They even started calling me Curious George the little monkey. I use to get so mad about that. They would say because I had little ears and they stuck out I looked like a little monkey. That had become one of the things I hated most. I had started school in Memphis. I went to Balmoral Elementary school. I had been suspended on my first day of school for pulling the fire alarm. What's really funny is my daughter did the exact same thing! East Memphis had been predominantly a white neighborhood in the 90's. My best friend named was White David. We called him White David because my brother David lived with us too and we use to get them mixed up. White David and his family was the first white family that I had ever met. It also was the first time I had been exposed to racism. He had the stereotypical white family. His father name was Guy. His mother acted nice but was racist as hell. His Dog was even racist but Guy was that guy. He was the one I guess suffered from White guilt because he made sure my grandmother had all the fruit and kept her yard clean etc. The wife was a low key freak she actually liked black people I guess the way I use to catch my cousin Deon sneaking out their house. He would be sneaking out the house from doing whatever with the wife and me and my cousin

Brittany would be sneaking out the garage from stealing all the ice cream and popsicles. White David and I would play all the time. I was always the robber and he was the cop. Back then the police would ride around the neighborhood and if you stopped them as a child they would give you a toy police badge. I had got one before but I always played a better bad guy or Villain. I was the robber or an Indian during Cow Boys and Indian's. I would go watch all the kids movies at White Davids house. Toy Story, Lion King you name it. He had all the best toys and things. I really loved being at his house. But I remember they had a daughter. She was a little older than me and I used to like her. She was my first white girl crush. I can reflect back on the time I had liked her so much I went to Balmoral Elementary School and had found my first white girlfriend. We had got caught during naptime dry-humping. I would get suspended so much in Elementary school to the point it was like I didn't even go to school. To give you a better look at the way my environment sort of shaped my mentality, I remember one day I had been snooping around my mother's room. My stepfather Rick had a loaded gun hid somewhere I can't remember exactly where, but I had found this gun. It was in a leather holster. I had been posing with this gun in the mirror as if I was this gangsta. I had even went as far as carrying the gun around the house. My cousin Carman had been downstairs watching her stories. Carman was in a wheelchair and a lot of the times she would be the one watching the kids if my grandmother was sleep or something. My grandmother rarely left us alone. But I had this big gun and I remember Carman sitting there watching her shows. I had snuck up behind her and pointed the gun to the back of her head and said, "break yo'self-fool!" So she obviously could feel the cold steel on the back of her neck and she instantly got scared and started yelling at me. She told on me so fast and I really didn't even realize that the gun was real and it was loaded. Man my mother, my grandmother, my stepfather and my grandfather beat me with belts, switches. Oh my grandfather whooping was the worst. He would make us go pick out twigs and he would braid them. It's ironic because my father's dad use to do the same thing. I'll touch on Mister A very soon. But yeah they beat my Butt! By the time I had reached the second grade my mother had moved to Marina Cove apartment complex. I had a bunk bed. Me and my brother share the room. My stepfather had married my mother and this was the moment they decided to create a household. Rick was a real nigga whether I felt that way as a child. He did a lot of thing that I later leaned on while doing time. I mean he put me thru some stuff but it was to make me strong because he knew I was going to be incarcerated when I had gotten old enough. Sad but it was true. I appreciated and valued those lessons now as a man.

Rick would be abusive mentally, physically and emotionally. He wasn't so much beating my mother, but he would beat her children. My brother David was smart though, he had caught on at an early age and went to live with my cousins. But back then every time I'd get suspended or something Rick would do things like make us sleep on the balcony during the wintertime. Or he would make us work out or just flat out whoop us. I was a straight A student in school. It wasn't the fact I wasn't able to pass, it was the fact I was just so problematic that the schools couldn't handle me. I use to think most of my mother fights with my stepfather was behind my actions because I was so bad. Onetime my mother and my stepfather had got into a physical altercation. He had apparently put his hands on my mother. My aunty Dorothy had been intown and she was for no games. Aunt Dottie was a real street nigga. She did it all. I'll touch more on aunty Dorothy later in my life story because she played a huge role as well. But I remember she had come over with a machine gun. I haven't never seen Rick so scared. Even after seeing that I watched my mother go back to him every time. I even seen them fight and someone would call the police on Rick. The police would show up and my mother would deny things ever happened and if the police didn't believe her she would fight with the police and both her and Rick would be locked up. Yeah, they had one of them type relationships. But here's where I would say Rick was a real nigga outside the b.s he did, but he'd always lose that real nigga moment. One day we had made a pact that if I bring back good grades he would get me some new shoes. So one day he had brought me a pair of Grant Hills. They were the black and green ones. I had just got them and I remember soon as Rick would get mad or fall out with my mother he'd take it out on me. So this nigga went and took the Grant Hills he had just bought me and threw them in the pond that encircled the complex. I cried so hard because I had thought we were just getting that stepfather/stepson bond. Rick seen how it affected me and decided to admit that he did me wrong and then gave me like three hundred dollars. Let me tell about that three hundred dollars though. I learned a huge lesson and to this day I don't let my mother get away with that. I was literally like six or seven years old and this event has followed me to my thirties. So after Rick had gave me the three hundred dollars, I was walking around with this wad of cash. My mother had approached me with a proposition. She told me to let her hold my money so that I wouldn't lose or spend it. So I'm like this my mother I can trust her with anything. So I gave her the money for safekeeping, however, one day I asked for some of the money if not all of it, I was shocked to find out that my mother spent all my money. From that day I haven't trusted my mother with any of my funds, however, later in my story that one action caused me to entrust other people who in turn had done the same exact thing to me. But we will get there. Around that time living in Marina Cove I had not only been a bad kid but I was also a bad influence on my cousins Brittany and Angie. Brittany and Angie are the only cousins on my mother's side of the family that's my age. So growing up I had only them to play with when I was little. All of my male cousins were too old for me to hang with or they was just never around for me to chill with them. So one day me and my two female cousins had been at my mother's apartment. Angie had just been in town from Detroit. My aunty Brenda was such a Detroiter she refused to move down south so we would see Angie during holidays or some special occasions. Brittany and I stayed in

Memphis. Now we had been deeply influenced by the Rug Rats cartoon. I was like Tommy and Angie was like Angelica and Brittany was like Lill. So I had this bright idea to go on this adventure like the characters did int he cartoons. I remember saying, "hey y'all wanna goon an adventure?" My cousins both had their own way of saying my name. For some reason it was hard fort hem to pronounce DeAngelo. So Brittany would call me "Ant'lo" and Angie would call me "An' joes", so they both like ," Adventure? An'joes 'Ant'lo' where we going to go?"

    Mind you I told you there was a pond that encircled the complex. So I'm like we can cross the rivers and our final destination would be Mc Donalds. They agreed and I led the way. We had reached the pond and it was this huge tree branch that stretched across to the other side of the pond. When we reached it I warned them of this 'sea monster' which just happened to be a Catfish or some domestic fish that just ended up in the pond. I remember seeing how big it was so I always thought it would eat me, so it went perfect with the narrative of this adventure (There goes my imagination again.) We crossed this huge tree branch. I think one of us slipped into the water that was actually no more that one or two feet. We could literally stand in the water. But it was exciting as hell. So we navigate ourselves around this complex. I honestly didn't know where we were at, I just played the part. We had been wondering around clueless. Somehow we ended up finding Mc Donalds and we were so happy. We played in the playpen filled with the balls and back then you could get them small ice cream cones and get free ice cream. I remember going for our third or fourth serving of the free ice cream and a lady had entered the Mc Donalds and seen me on my tippytoes trying to get the perfect swirl. She instantly collared me up like "your mother is looking for you! where is your cousins?!" I'm thinking LADY WHO IS YOU? The Lady packed us in her car with her two kids after ordering their food and took us to our mothers. Man soon as I walked into the house both my cousins like, "it was An'joes idea!" They got whooped but they beat my behind as usual. My mother could not sit still. Her and my stepfather moved like Gypsies. We moved to Knight Way Apartments. This complex was where I really accepted the fact that I was just always going to be a bad kid. I remember I use to get my hair cut by Big Jay. Big Jay later became my cousin Tiffany husband and children's Father. Big Jay was my first big homie ever. He had been in the streets heavy back in the day. I use to go down to his apartment with my mother's permission to get my hair cut and he would be giving me game like I was his age or something. I had to been in the second grade around this time. He knew me before my stepfather even befriended him and before he'd became my barber. He would watch me bully the other kids around the complex. I remember my friend Little Kenny had this red Corvette power wheel. Me and Kenny used to fight for the leadership position amongst the other kids. I ended up being better with the hands and became the little leader. I would make Kenny and the other kids push me around the complex in the Power Wheel Corvette. The Power Wheels battery had died out so we had to get around in it somehow right? Big Jay use to be out doing his daily thug I would say and he always admired the fact I was the littlest out the pack but was the head honcho. He started calling me Lil Nino. I never knew who Nino was until later in life after seeing New Jack City. I guess the fact New Jack City was based on some group out of Detroit despite being shot in New York, I reminded him of Nino Brown whether it was by the way I had the kids following me or the way I carried myself. It's like he knew I'd be somebody with hood or street status when I got older. I lived up to some of those things Nino did but Later in life I found out Nino Brown was a rat and never embraced that moniker again. But with that nickname I was finally somebody in the hood. I had my own identity that the big homies gave me. I told people that was my name in school, all in the complex, everywhere. Plus I had beat Kenny up and I started beating all the other kids up who thought they were the tuff guys. I wouldn't say I was a bully though I did exert my influence but I felt I earned it to be with the bad guys. I had everybody in school scared of me and low key even the guys I was actually scared of had joined me. So I had the bullies with me and I was acknowledged by the big homies. So my Lil name was mentioned among my peers big brothers or cousins and nobody messed with me. With all bad attributes came the down side. Every time something happened in the complex or even among my siblings I would be blamed. It got to the point I just didn't care and started really being bad. I remember I had convinced my stepbrothers Jeremi, Arlandis, and their older cousins following me to steal. We had went to Toys R' Us and stole all kinds of BB Guns and things of that nature. One of the cousins ended up not meeting us at our meeting spot. So while we waited for him I was playing with a book of matches. I would strike them and toss them assuming they'd burn out. However, the field had caught fire and on top of that my step cousin got caught stealing and he told on us because the police had been looking for us. By time they got to us the Fire Department was there too. Since I didn't get caught with any stolen items the fireman decided to take me to my parents. Man this big guy had me by the collar three feet off the ground, feet dangling and he said to my mother, "is this your son?!" That was the first time I had ever had any police/authority encounter. As time went on my mother had decided to move back home to Detroit, Michigan. My stepfather obviously got tired of my grandmother and the family getting in his family business. However, my grandmother had me stay with her and my brother David stayed with my cousin Tiffany. My mother ultimately didn't have a choice because my grandmother threatened to call the state. So my mom's went back with just my sister who is Rick biological daughter.

    My grandmother had moved twice before we landed in South Memphis where we lived up until my grandfather passed away. White Haven also known by its black residents as "Black Haven." Black Haven was where I really jumped off the porch. We stayed on Shelby Drive and Hill Brook road. Black Haven was that neighborhood you'd kind of see on T.V when they displayed Memphis. It wasn't too far from Elvis Presley's mansion and The Heartbreak Hotel. This neighborhood had real southern hospitality. Because I still spoke with a northern accent, people called me

IN DIS CELL DEANGELO ANTHONY

Little Detroit. After attending White Haven Elementary School where my cousin was the principal, I went to Geeter Middle School. Black Haven was a rough neighborhood. I had to fight nearly every day with them county boys. I would always get made fun of because my accent. They would say I sounded liked MX. I'm like I'm not even from New York but okay. I thought I was really tough as Nino in East Memphis but I quickly learned that there's always someone bigger and badder. I had a hard time finding friends honestly but I had been cool with a couple guys from the neighborhood that embraced me like family. Suga Lump and Mane was my guys. They both was known to be about that action. Every time I got into any beefs I'd call them and they'd show up and help me fight. They called it' Jacking'.Lump for short was really the ring leader. He first introduced me to gang activity. He was a Lord and his brother Muu Muu was one of their leaders. Mane had been a Lord too. So I really had been educated on Chicago Organizations. I would attend their meetings some times and I first wanted to be apart of the Lords but I would see how Muu Muu would finesse his subordinates out their money as if he was collecting dues but spent them doing other things. I had started carrying guns back then too because Lump was beefing with everybody in the hood. As the time went on I had gained a name for myself and had respect from people outside my normal circle. I was Little Detroit and I would go around sticking my chest out. I had met my first real girlfriend named Jaricka. Jaricka was my cousin Brittany friend. We all went to Geeter Middle School. Jaricka was my first love. She had so much love and respect for me to the point my grandmother used to allow her to stay over at our house. My grandfather had built an extension to our three bedroom house. He added on to the house and it was like we had a baby mansion. So it was so many places me and Jaricka would duck off to and make out. I didn't lose my virginity with her. I actually kinda of skipped pass that part but I had lost my virginity with a girl from my grandmother's church. Mind you I told you my grandmother had the juice and as a pastor her congregation would come to her house to pray and help around the house. One of the sisters daughter would come over and we'd sneak off. Back to Jaricka. So one day me and Jaricka had been in the back room where my cousin Deon stayed. We had finally had sex. She was built like a grown woman. I had never seen or smelled that natural scent of a woman. We had both basked in each other's company until my grandmother caught us. She was like, "What's that I smell? I smell sex! You cotton pickin' nigga get that girl out of here!" She looked at Jaricka and said, "you alt' to be ashamed of yourself little girl!" Jaricka from that day never came back around and I never seen her again. But the reason I brought Jaricka up was because I had met a young country boy who turned out to be one of my best friends and biggest influence. Jareeko was a twin. His twin had been dating Jarickas older sister and somehow we met and became cool. Now this part of my life story is very important because later in this story, this very story happened to be what created the most difficult chapter in my life during my incarceration. So Jareeko was around twelve years old. I want to say we both were the same age or I had him by a month or so.

Jareeko was already deep in the gang culture at that age. He was smoking weed and doing whatever he wanted to do. His father sold drugs, and his older brother was one of the leaders of the Locs set in Black Haven. Jareeko had basically been raised up to be a Loc and he was my best friend. I would hang with him and do all the things he did growing up. Everybody he fought I fought. He went to the skating ring I went. He had influenced me so much that I had started wearing some of the same clothes he had. Jareeko and his twin had all their friends representing the group however, I was not willing to allow three guys to jump me into the gang. I witnessed one of their initiations one day and they beat the kid up so bad and I never wanted to go through that process. I was more guilty by association than anything. Black Haven was home to two major gangs. You had the Locs and then the Lords. They shared their territory or turf and symbolized their union by wearing one of two colors; Purple or Gold. Most guys wore them together. They would team up if other neighborhoods tried to come around and they would fight each other every now and then as well.

    So I'm hanging with Jareeko and guys started identifying me as a Loc. Only me and the Locs I hung with knew I was never put on their set. Even my Lord homeboys started assuming I was a Loc. However, to be honest I was a Lord technically because I was going through the process when I hung with Lump and his brothers. At that time being a Loc was cool. You had all the west coast rappers spreading their lifestyle through the music and I had family that was Locs as well. Then you had guys C-walking and doing all that. I had started claiming to be a Loc and no one ever challenged the fact whether I was official or not. I was just a kid though and never really had no idea of what it meant to be a Loc. Things had gotten bad once everybody started identifying me as a Loc. I had fought so many guys because of my association with Jareeko. Funny thing everybody we had beef with was other Loc sets that had been around the City of Memphis. It was hundreds of Locs sets around Memphis then. You'd rarely see a Damu back when I lived there. One day I had been at my grandmother house chilling with my cousin Brittany. Brittany had a friend that went to school with us. This girl was so disrespectful to me to the point I called her out her name and she swung on me. When she swung I just blacked out and punched her. Bad decision. It was something about all these attributes that I inherited and never chose for myself that sort of guided me through life. I remember walking to my friend Jareeko house. He stayed in this gated community known as Long Manner Gardens. People called them the LMG's because it was a local neighborhood gang that dominated that community. So I'm walking through the LMG's with my head up like I was that Guy. Fights were big in Memphis. They didn't do any shooting too much when I was a kid there but fights was their thing. I remember a crowd of kids walking up towards me as I crossed the parking lot of this plaza. I see these kids with their flags out they left pockets and they were in all black. One kid started taking his shirt off and this girl was pointing towards me. I had just gotten out of school, I got my backpack on all type of stuff. It was like all the kids but me knew it was about to be a brawl and I was one of the contenders. When I realized that it was my cousin friend pointing at me, I knew then because the kid didn't hesitate to get on me. He swung me around the lot like a ragdoll. He didn't give me a chance to even throw a punch. He was punching, kicking and stumping me out with a few other kids. They beat me down bad and instead of continuing my trip through the LMG's I turned back around and ran home. My grandmother seen how they had lumped me up and had me bleeding from the nose and lip. I went and tossed my backpack in my room and headed for the door. My grandmother tried to stop me I pushed pass her and ran up the block to go get my big homie Suga Lump. As I said before, Lump was willing to fight all my battles because he seen me as his little brother. Lump got his bike. It was just me and him. That's how gangster Lump was he didn't get a group or his gang like he could have, it was me and him. He was known to carry a gun though. But the kids that beat me up was still hanging around the plaza as if they anticipated me to come back. I mean the whole crowd was there spectators and all. When we arrived I jumped off the handlebars and Lump dropped his bike. Everybody knew he wasn't the one to be messed with and he was great with the hands. Come to find out the kid that beat me up was a highschoolers and Lump knew exactly who they were. He called him out instantly. I stood aside as ordered and watched Lump beat this kid down. He beat him up so bad that I ended up pulling Lump off him. The kids the other guy was with had ran up and Lump upped his chrome pistol like, "Wass' Up mane?" he spoke so country. When I got home my grandmother and grandfather was waiting on me. They all out on the front lawn. The kid Lump beat up had apparently already came to the house looking for me. I didn't know. But after this fight my grandmother had enough of my mess. She said I was into a gang and she feared me being killed or something. I'm like "Gang? I'm not in no Gang butokay."CHAPTER:3 In Dis Cell (Most of My Life)"Detroit-Detroit! That's The City I Claim/ On Stage Fifty Thousand People Screaming My Name."-Blade Ice wood Detroit, Michigan seemed so right to me. I felt at home. There was just something about being back in the city I was born in. My mother and my stepfather had owned a two-family flat on the east side of Detroit. We had lived near the City Airport on St. Patrick's and Conners. I had been enrolled in Cooper Elementary which was a great school if you asked me. Growing up on the east side of Detroit was where I had begun to see life without that veil over my eyes. It was like living in a third world country. However, not so much where we lived. I'm speaking on certain parts like Rohns and Lambert or Georgia and Helen. It was so much going on in the city of Detroit. The murder rate had been so high. But for children it was really something maturing about it. I had started actively having girlfriends. I was skipping school in elementary. I did do great as far as curriculum. I passed every class. Of course I was always getting suspended.

CHAPTER 3 In Dis Cell (Most of My Life)

I remember getting off the school bus and that walk up the block. I use to be tuff as nails on the bus. I had guys like Ice wear Vezzo (Chavez), Rich Boy (Ralph) as well as, my little cousins Juan-Juan around me. Between guys of their ilk you couldn't show no weaknesses. But that walk home to face momma after that suspension...Man it was terrible. I really didn't respect my mother's whippings. She would whip me with a belt but I'd act like I was crying. Overtime my stepfather peeped that those whippings didn't phase me, so they agreed to allow him to discipline me. Boy was that the wrong thing my mother could've agreed too. Now I was back in the hands of Rick and he was for no games. Before my stepbrothers moved to Detroit from Atlanta, I was the only focus. One day I had done something and Rick decided that I should be confined to the closet in the living room. True story. So I'm confined to this closet and the purpose was to get me to behave because I was heading towards some form of incarceration in his eyes. Was it right? No! However, I remember I ended up embracing the confinement and made the best of it. One night Rick came home and went to check on me in the closet and he found that I had turned the walk-in closet into some clubhouse. This was where my imagination had protected me mentally. I was always numb to abuse honestly because I would escape mentally to this imaginary world. I had extension cords running along the walls into the closet, where I had this jelly dolphin nightlight plugged in. I had made like a sleeping bag. I had pillows all fluffed up and comfortable looking. I even had a stash of snacks and the few action figures I did own. Poke' Mon cards were a big thing back then. I had hundreds of those cards playing by myself. To Rick I was having too much fun. So he snatched the cords from the wall, tossed my nightlight against the wall and made me hand over all the items I used for entertainment. Even after taking everything and enforcing it with my mother not to let me sneak out the closet almost not even to use the bathroom, I found some paper and made football's, playing with them like I had real toys. As I started to get in my teens and attended middle school Rick realized there was nothing he could do to change who I was. I went to Burghs Middle school. This school was lawless. It was like the school in the movie Cooley High. I'd be trying to get some in the back stairwells of the gym, or shooting dice between the thresholds of the cafeteria. If I wanted to really have fun all you had to do was go to detention. Detention was like a party. Back then there was this program that had been implemented in the schools called Black Family Development. So detention was in the counselors office. All the popular girls was there. The bad guys had all the good girls. I remember sitting in detention with like three or four girls I had already dated. Burghs was such a bad school and known for teachers getting shot and robbed. They found people dead all kind of things. The superintendent ended up closing the school down later after my eight grade year. As I adapted to my environment, I became popular in my neighborhood. I was known for running with my friends

Ralph and the older guys in the hood. My big homies use to get me drunk and high we'd be in the car messed up. I had first started rapping then. I remember Freeway album had been one of the hottest albums that year. My big homie Low and John use to get me to freestyle. I had to be good at it because they never not wanted to have me in their ciphers. I had to be like twelve/thirteen years old. The older guys loved having me around and I would blend right in. So I was getting all the game from them and I'd go back and teach all the younger kids around the neighborhood. Man I was so funny back then! I had practiced martial arts growing up. Low key I learned it from Rick. So I use to watch too many Bruce Lee and Three Ninjas movies apparently because I would have ten kids in the basement teaching them martial arts. We even sometimes practiced in my front yard. I had the kimono and a yellow belt. I'm out there with a row of kids following all my instructions. The older guys in the hood started calling me Master DeAngelo. Real talk. I laughed to myself even remembering these events. I had been hosting fights in my mother's basement way before UFC was a sport. Some of the kids that wasn't so tough would run home to their parents and tell on us for beating them up. I mean I had kids damn near four to ten years old bare knuckle boxing in the basement. I'm sure I taught a lot of those kids how to defend themselves growing up. In fact I've ran into a few of them in prison and was proud to see how they were able to survive without being a victim or cowards. I had earned quite the name on The Six. I knew everybody from Flanders's all the way back to McNickels. Most of the baddest females around my age I had either been cool with. Everything that I was on growing up down south, I had brought with me to Detroit. I did the wanna be gang member stuff and all. I was such a bad influence on my stepbrothers. I had always got us in trouble. Jeremi to this day is my biggest supporter and best friend. I had him doing everything I did. One day his father had did us so bad. I can't remember exactly what we did but he punched Jeremi and beat me with the belt. He used the belt on me because around that time I knew that my grandmother, and aunts on both my mother/fathers side of the family would come to my rescue. I remember looking at my stepbrother Jeremi after his father beat him up and was like, "bro let's kill this nigga?"

We devised a plan to grab the lighter fluid we had in the back staircase and I went to my big homies to geta gun. The plan was to wait until my mother went to work, and when Rick was sleep I was going to shoot him and Jeremi was to set the bed on fire. SMH, terrible kid. We use to climb from the front top porch, across the roof and down the back porch. So I sneak out the night of and went and grabbed the pistol from one of my guys. I had been given a chrome .22 Caliber pistol. I had hid the gun under the back porch. I had to wait until like four in the morning to sneak back inside the house because my mother would be back home and Rick always woke up. I spent a lot of my time at my girlfriends motherhouse. Her mother was cool with my mom's so I could go over there anytime. My mother just didn't know I snuck out every night to go hang with my girlfriend. Anyhow, I waited to go back home but I ended up oversleeping at my girlfriend house. Now since I had overslept I missed the window of opportunity to execute the plan, but I also got caught for sneaking out. When I made it in the house I remember thinking like WHY IS A POLICE CAROUTSIDE THE HOUSE? MAY BE MY MOMS CALLEDTHE POLICE BECAUSE I SNUCK OUT? I never assumed or anticipated the fact that ain't no way in hell was I going to get my stepbrother to murder his father with me no matter how he treated us. The police had been standing in the front room waiting on me. They had the gun I had in a evidence bag and my mom stared at me with her arms folded in pure disappointment. I remember the police calling an ambulance to the house and instead of taking me to jail I was taken to the mental house. I can't remember exactly which one because I had been to them all by the time I was twelve, but I want to say I was at Kingwood's Hospital. This was when my family and the state started to really pay attention to my mental health. I had already went through the ADHD, ADD, Rid land stage. They was thinking more like bipolar and having a serious mood disorder. I had been medicated and forced stay and participate in the group counseling. I had tried to rebel once and they restrained me and injected something that put me straight to sleep. From that point mental health became a huge part of my life. After trying to get Rick killed I think my mother and him agreed that maybe I should live with someone else. My mother figured she'd give my father side of the family a shot. My aunt Felisha had already moved in the family flat below us, however they had moved on Gratiort and Semore. We stayed in this neighborhood for a while up until my cousins got into it with the neighbor's below our two family flat. I remember I overheard an argument with them between my cousin Michelle and some other female. Not sure why they had such heated dispute, but I'm so overprotective with my female cousins to the point my bad behind took water balloons filled with bleach in them and I threw them from the top porch on to the neighbor's. Why did I do that? Man they charged up the stairs trying to kick our door in. We was so scared. My aunty and her husband wasn't home then so we called them. Julian wasn't no joke. He was a boxer and he kept a pistol or two. So they stopped whatever they were doing and rushed home. Julian had a luxury car. It looked like a Cadillac to me. The white Cadillac looking vehicle pulled up and there was like a twenty minute pause before they finally made it up to the house. Whatever Julian and my aunt did or said the neighbor's didn't want any smoke. There was definitely guns drawn. As always though, fingers pointed at me for dropping the balloons. Only this time I was praised for trying to stand up for my family. See The Anthony Family is/was very close. My father's siblings had so many children as well. So that made it where I could be all over the city of Detroit. My father is originally from the East side. They grew up on Rohm's and Gratiort. If you paid any attention to my stories about my father's side of the family, you'd see that when it came to unity especially against adversaries, we came together. I could be way on the westside of Detroit minding my own business and the kids off Rohns could be about to fight with some kids across Harper or wherever, my uncle Michael would round up all his nephews and nieces so we can help his friends children fight some other kids. I remember one day acting like I wasn't going to help them fight, man my uncle and his homeboy's would stretch me out by the arms and legs, then punch me multiple times in my chest. They didn't believe in being a coward. I had finally had an opportunity to meet my father for the second time a lot earlier then where I'm at in the story. I wanted to tell you the story from all points of views where you get to see the family as a whole. So my first time meeting my father I had to be like three or something. I just remember going to Jackson Penitentiary and being in the visiting room playing with this little wooden car. I had went with my grandmother Naomi on my father's side. While my father was locked up outside that we rarely had communication. Only thing I had to connect with my father during his entire incarceration was some hobby craft material and an alarm clock shaped as a motorcycle helmet.

    My father had finally been paroled and he immediately came to get me. He had won a law suit before he got home on Ionia Maximum Security Prison for their inhumane treatment of him, so he had a nice little start. He had lived with his girlfriend in Bright more, Michigan right outside Detroit city limits. I must admit during that time period in my life my pops tried to raise me but something's are just inevitable. I was still bad as hell, I was stealing from stores and running the neighborhood. I attended Thomas Holton Elementary my second grade year. I remember I had skipped school with the girls that lived next door to me. I remember the smell of roaches that seemed to cover the walls. These roaches were so gangsta they would be out moving around freely during the day, and like they were attending a club at night. I remember being spotted by one of the neighbors stopping at these girls house. It was so stupid because we lived right next door to them and all our neighbors were so nosey. Plus, my auntie Felisha had lived directly across the street with my cousins Jasmine and Katherine. We all went to school together as well. I'm not sure who dimed me out honestly, but I do recall that being the first time my father ever put his hands on me. My pops really didn't like disciplining me with a belt. He tried to whip me that day I could see how bad he felt. I think I cried simply because it was so hard for him to hit me. After that he tried other forms of discipline such as holding books, pushups and writing words out the dictionary a hundred times. Possibly why I became so articulate if I do say so myself. As time went on this form of discipline had become the norm. Whippings didn't affect me. I had mastered the art of fake crying. Thus, it seemed that not only did my father implement such discipline, my stepfather Rick did as well. Just when my father was striving to be back in my life, he had been arrested once again for violation of parole. I was told later in life that his girlfriend at the time had falsely reported something that had gotten him back incarcerated. When I was a kid I assumed he had just abandoned me once again. It was that stereotypical abandonment, you know the one where the kid is sitting on the porch waiting for his father? Well I literally experienced exactly that. My pops was supposed to take me to see my cousins at my grandparents' house but never showed up. As I recall, the woman that my father was in a relationship with had tried to kidnap me. My aunty Brenda had come and retrieved me. I was so happy to see her pulling up to the curb in her little Honda. I was being mentally and physically abused by the woman that had me. To be thoroughly honest, I believe at one point her son had made homosexual passes at me. He had a huge collection of action-figurers that I use to love to play with, and one day he had told me if I'd give him fellatio I didn't have to ask permission to play with the toys. I remember thinking like that can't be right? I remember threatening to tell my father on him. Good thing he had played it off as if he was just joking but thinking back as I write this story of mind I believe if I would've fell for the banana in the tail pipe he would've molested me. Thus, my aunt Brenda rescued me from having to experience being molested by another man. Sadly, I couldn't go back home to live with my mother due to my stepfather being abusive. I had went to live at my grandparents' house on Schoolcraft and Rutherford. Mr. and Mrs. "A" didn't play! I think that's the only household I lived in where I behaved myself. My grandparents both didn't hold any of the grandchildren up. We had to eat properly at the dinner table, you couldn't leave the table until you've eaten everything on the plate. Oh, and don't even think putting sugar in your rice. We had to do choirs the whole nine. All-in-all my grandparents were very good people. They literally fed the entire neighborhood. My grandfather Mr. Anthony would BBQ for the whole block. Everybody had respect for my family. We kept the neighborhood clean and it wasn't a time I could ever say I've seen someone disrespect my grandparents. They'd sit on the porch all day smoking their cigarettes. My grandparents took pride in their lawn, the grass was the greenest of the greenest. We bet not had gotten caught dead on their lawn it would've been a sad day in hell. But I loved them same as my mother's parents. I was always my grandparents favorite if you asked me. They seemed to realize that as a child I needed extra love and affection. I had attended Edison Elementary school with my cousins. The school at the time was a very good school. They had great teachers and despite it being almost mandatory that you learned something at school with my grandparents, the school made learning fun to me. I had gotten good grades and never got suspended from school. The holidays was the best at my grandparents' house. My uncles would come from Atlanta with tons of fireworks on the Fourth of July. It was like a ritual. Every year they would put on an elaborate show for the neighborhood. It was almost better than the fireworks downtown Detroit. After they'd set the block on fire, we would eat good and just enjoy family moments. It was some of the best times of my life honestly. I use to wish my father was there to experience things with us. Everybody pitched in to show me and my brother David love on behalf of my father. It was a feeling that I couldn't find elsewhere. My mother's side of the family had that same love but some of my aunts treated me like the black sheep of the family. I wasn't alone though, my cousin Brittany was

IN DIS CELL DEANGELO ANTHONY

Not to go off course but I wanted to just show you what I mean by being treated as the black sheep. One of my aunts on my mother's side that I love dearly had a funny way of showing me love. I must have been so bad to her that she had made a room in her basement that she named "Hell's Kitchen." Hell's Kitchen was quite hilarious if you think about it. I know it sounds crazy, but it was an actual place at her house. It was in the laundry room where she had a second kitchen. In the kitchen there was a round table with a stuffed red devil hanging from the light fixture. If you acted bad you'd serve like a time out. They were so religious to the point they implemented this sort of fear into the children. I wasn't spooked at all. Well, after I've spent so much time in this room with this stuffed red devil, I realized that it was a scare tactic. Once my aunty seen those tactics didn't affect me, she went as far as leaving me behind while all the other cousins went to Disney Land and Six Flags! I never was able to go on these family vacations. My mother even used to be mad about that. It was sad because to this day I never got the chance to go to such huge amusement park that every kid in the world wanted to experience. The closest I got to a Six Flags or Disney Land was the State Fair and Cedar Point.

"As a parent we only want what's best for ourchildren."- Superbadd37.I remember the day our last U-Haul had left St. Patrick's street. I could see all my friends sadly waving farewell. My little sister had tears rolling down her cheeks. My mother had a sigh of relief as she made her way up Gratiort crossing 8 Mile road into East Detroit. My mother had rented a two bedroom apartment on 9 Mile and Schaner. The tenement building was nice and clean. It was a very quiet neighborhood for the most part. My cousin Faith had lived in the unit next to where we lived, her and her daughter. There was this grocery store right next door which made everything quite accessible and it made the perfect environment to raise a happy family so my mother thought. We lived between East Point and Warren Michigan which was a predominantly white neighborhood back in 2003. There was only like ten minority residents that I knew of and my family was of the tenth. I had been enrolled at Oakwood Middle School. Oakwood was literally right around the block from our apartment building. I remember my first day of school. I had to take a picture for a school I'd something you'd never experience at that time in Detroit Public School systems. I had my little G-Unit Ecko shirt on and some Paco shorts. I was so mad at my mother for buying me some cheap clothing but I was a team player and I knew we had to cut back after her and my stepfather split. We went from hitting the mega millions to barely making ends meet but my mother always made it happen. She didn't care how hard she'd have to work she never allowed her fronts to be down. She made sure her children was clean clothed, her house was decorated and she kept a nice vehicle. She did her best and a lot of those characteristics followed me my entire life. I had become one of the few black kids in the neighborhood that roamed freely. At school I was real popular because the other kids could tell that I wasn't from their neck of the woods. I was a Detroit baby and that came with a lot of stereotypes that my actions gave life to. I was always tough, mean and ready to exude violence. I never really had too many beefs with the kids around the neighborhood except for these white kids that claimed to be apart of a Neo-Nazi. I remember my first encounter with these kids. I was walking through the neighborhood with my friend Jeremy Roundtree and we would go around stealing trick-bikes. We knew some females that we would go smoke weed with and just chill if we didn't find any kind of bikes we wanted. We went for the Dino GTs, Mongoose etc. So as we walked up this block there was a group of older white guys listening to rock music and drinking beers. We didn't really think much of it especially because we were kids and they had to be way older than we were. Plus we never stole anything off this block because we hung out on their street. As we approached the house were the females normally be at, one of the white guys had yelled loud as he could as a means to scare us. We paid him no mind because they were already loud and obnoxious when we arrived. Plus, we didn't make out anything he had said until he had repeated it clearly, "THE WHITEMAN MARCHES ON!!"The females had exited the front door inviting us in as usual. They had all kinds of beer and liquor. We had hit the weed bong and listened to Triple Six' Mafia. As we were just minding our own business one of the girls had went to the door and let in some white kid around our age. He had come in dressed like some punk rocker with white shoelaces and chains hanging from his ripped shorts. The kid had seemed to have a chip on his shoulder because I remember nodding to him and he completely shunned me like I wasn't even there but I didn't care. The kid sat down on the couch L-shape from where we had sat. The two females that we would normally make out with and take to the backrooms was on our sides doing our normal thing. The kid had bolted tohis feet as if he was angry about us kissing on the other girls and stormed outside to the porch. The girl that had let him in followed behind him. The music was so loud we couldn't hear exactly what they were saying but that was the least of our concerns at that point

    The female had come back into the house and turned down the music. She shifted her hips and said, "hey Zack's mad he said he doesn't appreciate our company." I looked around and laughed because we would be at this house every day and never had anyone say anything out the way to us. Jeremy on the other hand wasn't feeling that. He had lived in this neighborhood way longer than I and he had experienced racism quite often. He knew exactly what the kid was trying to say. Jeremy was a fighter. He didn't care who you were, how big or bad you were he always stood his ground. I just remember peering out the window seeing a group of bald husky white guys with chains, bats and beer bottles marching toward the house. I'm like, AWWMAN! "What y'all want to do?!" Jeremy yelled out dashing towards the front door. I can't lie I was so scared because I never had to experience nothing like that with white people. I been called the N word etc. but not hated enough to where we would be assaulted for being black in the neighborhood my mother paid her due tax dollars to live in. I grabbed Jeremy trying my best to hold him back.

Jeremy was a lot bigger than me and stronger but I seemed to had all the strength in the world that day. One of the white girls was on the phone with 911yelling frantically. "Hurry up the guys across the street are coming to attack my friends!" she made sure the guys could hear and see her on the phone with the police. East Point police station was literally a block away from their home. Thus, the group of guys had begun to back off when they witnessed her calling the cops. Honestly, after I had experienced that event I stopped going to go visit the females we had hung with. I would see them at school and the was about it. I had started trying to find other friends and hangout spots in the neighborhood. There was these older Arab guys that had twin Mustang 5.0's. They had hung with a few white guys that acted black. The white guys drove old school Chevy's sitting on rims. They was cool and I was like their little black homie. They also loved Triple 6' Mafia and the Memphis, Tennessee culture and I had related to them based on that. They listened to all the classics and was shocked to find out I knew all the songs and I knew how to Jook like Country Black so they all started calling me Lil Country. It was funny because little did they know I was from across 8 Mile but I went along with it because it was hard finding friends of their stature. I would be with them all the time riding around smoking, drinking and flexing in their pimped outrides. I would be able to stay at their houses playing video games and eating all kind of snacks. They really had love for me and at that point being sort of traumatized by the experience with the Neo-Nazi group, I needed to see that all white people wasn't racist as they made it seem. I had been hanging around one day with my older friends and they had introduced me to my home boy Keith Parish. Me and Keith clicked instantly. He was an Italian kid that had swag and related to the hood because he would go hang around in the city on Seven Mile and Hoover with some of the Bloods in the red zone. He even claimed to be a Blood which was funny to me because at that time I never knew that European descendants could join black street gangs. However, he made it believable because he stayed wearing the color red and repping the gang without fear of repercussions. Keith and I became real close. He was a true hustler as well. In fact I never actually had been properly introduced to the drug game until I met him. Though we were young, his father was a part of a biker gang and they had their hands on every drug you could name. We would be at Keith house breaking down pounds of marijuana, cutting and mixing cocaine. We would play with his father's guns. His father had an arsenal. I guess back then his father was running guns as well because we used to see boxes of firearms brand new in the box. I had already been smoking weed but I started experimenting with harder drugs when I started hanging with Keith. Keith would always be like, "yo'Country let's go tripping balls bro." (White boy voice) I had learned that tripping balls in the suburban slang meant snorting cocaine, staying up all hours of the 'morning'. I was popping ecstasy pills and next thing you know I was snorting lines of coke like a seventies movie. However, that cocaine trip was shortly lived for me because I didn't like the way it made my nose burn and I had already had complications with nosebleeds when I was younger but I did keep popping ecstasy pills. Yeah, Keith was a bad influence on my life but those were some of the funniest days of my life. Being able to have our hands on drugs in middle school made us gods. Keith had attended Kelly Middle school and I would sell drugs at Oakwood and all the females would flock to us. One female that I had come to be very close with was my friend Tamara. Tamara was a Latina of Mexican descent and her mother and father owned a two family flat down the street from my mother's apartment. Tamara lived upstairs by herself and she would host all kind of little parties where I would sell the drugs I'd get from Keith on consignment.

Tamara and I just clicked. I loved being around her. She was so beautiful and I had always wanted to haven Latina girlfriend. The first Latina I have ever dated was when I lived in Memphis and I didn't know the first thing about being in a relationship. But me and Tamara just had those vibes. I loved her attitude. She was very spicy and down-to-earth. All the girls in the neighborhood was terrified of her and wanted to be around her. I had ended up dating her friend Brittany first but I didn't necessarily like Brittany as much as I liked her sister. Jasmine was really my favorite girlfriend ever. Funny thing though we were babies. I was turning 14yrs old and she had just turned 13. Her mother and her mother's boyfriend loved me dearly. Jasmine was mixed. Her mother was white and her father was black. She had been this little defiant little girl with this long brown curly hair with freckles. She smoked like a chimney and we would get drunk off Captain Morgan. Yeah we were bad as hell. Our parents basically accepted the fact that we would be juvenile delinquents. Me and Jasmine fought like we were a married couple too. One day I had cheated on her with this white girl. I remember it like it was yesterday, my mother had caught me and the girl 'doing-it' in my room. I thought she was going to be working late instead she ended up coming home early. She cursed me and the girl out. I had went and told Tamara about it and Tamara dimed me out to Jasmine. Boy was she a hater for that. That's when I realized that Tamara really actually liked me but we didn't know how to initiate that connection. We just knew exactly how to destroy each other's relationships though. Life had taken a huge turn for me around this time. I had been involved in so many things a child should not have been involved in. Outside of what I have exposed to you, I had started doing Breaking-&-Entering's. A friend and I would go inside people's homes with little mettle-detector searching for firearms and jewelry. One of my friends father would purchase all the stolen goods and we would blow the money. Honestly, thinking back on how much money we would get it was like we were being robbed. Onetime we had went over some guys house that we had met stealing bikes. They had invited us to their home. We went over and smoked weed with them and played the PlayStation. My friend and I had this routine we do, we would take turns distracting the guy we were playing to rob while the other either stole things right then, or we just case out the house and come back. This particular house we had robbed had been a treasure trove. The guys parents we ex-military and they owned a bunch of handguns and hunting rifles. We were so far out in

IN DIS CELL DEANGELO ANTHONY

Macomb county that it would've been crazy to come back and try an steal all the guns, so we had ended up taking a few guns hoping that they wouldn't realize until it was too late. Plus we didn't really know the guys the we were stealing from so we figured we would get away with it. We ended up getting the guns and we stole a few bikes on the way home. I remember after dropping the guns off at Tamara house, I rode the bike with my friend halfway home so he could get home with the guns he had stolen. On my way back to Tamara's house I'd normally take the long way around, however, there was a short cut that you could take that was crossing the Oakwood Middle school football field to 9 Mile. It had been around 9pmon that summer night that I peddled thru the neighborhood. I had approached the block that we use to chill at with the other girls that had the Neo-Nazi group and unbeknownst to me, I was being followed by a pickup truck. I had stopped to lite a cigarette and three white guys jumped out the cab of the truck with mettle baton's yelling out, "get that nigger!" I almost urinated my pants. I jumped off the bike I had stolen miles from where we were and bolted up the side street, jumping a few gates and hiding alongside a yard shed until the coast was clear. I was gasping for air, scared as heck peaking around hoping that the guys were gone. Lucky me I was fast enough to get away because the baton's they had shot out from the handle and had like a ball point on the ends of them. So now I'm walking home cautiously. I headed for the short cut on feet and I just happened to look up and see a kid skateboarding on the side of the school. At first I didn't recognize the figure on the skateboard but I made out the clothing that he was wearing. It was one of the white guys that had chased me with the batons. I immediately started looking around as I ducked between the brush. I noticed he was by himself and I knew I could take him. I jumped from behind the brush yelling, "aye ShaneI got you now!" Soon as he seen the light reflect off my face he jumped the gate tossing his skateboard behind him. I walked up laughing feeling like I was superior over him an his ideology. I had already been known to beat racist guys up. Word was I had caught one guy weeks before this event and made him bite the curb like the white guy did in the movie American History X for calling me the N word. So Shane had knew that he didn't have a win with me whatsoever. I remember picking up the skateboard and trying to kick and push up the sidewalk towards 9 Mile, but I could barely stand on the skateboard so I tossed it and headed to Tamara's house for the night.

    That following morning I just remember hearing the fear and worry in Tamara's mothers voice as she woke up the entire house, "DE Angelo your mothers here and the police is looking for you?" All I could think was WHAT THE HECK ARE THEY LOOKING FORME FOR? My mother had been parked outside in her red FordF150 with a look I never seen on her face before. She had my sister in the passenger seat. My sister Me on even looked scared like they seen a ghost or something. I had got in the truck and my mother explained what had taken place that morning. The East Point Police had kicked in our apartment door guns drawn making my baby sister and mother get on their knees at gunpoint. They had torn the apartment up claiming that they were looking for a firearm and a robbery suspect. My mother was clueless, as well as I but they had been convinced that I had attempted to rob while armed the white guy Shane for a freaking skateboard. Yeah, the one I couldn't even ride. I was so baffled and shocked that they had done all this and I wouldn't even thought I'd be a robbery suspect. I had been told that I had to go in for questioning and my mother kept asking me if I did it as we pulled into the police station. I continued to say "no that's not what happened. "I had been questioned by an officer named Detective Mc Glockin and he was as racist as it gets. He told my mother he would get me looked up until I'm old enough to purchase liquor if I didn't admit to the allegations. I didn't admit to anything because I didn't do it. In fact at that time didn't any black kid skateboard that I knew of and if anyone should've been at question it should've been the white guys that had chased me and tormented the black kids around the neighborhood with their Neo-Nazi ideologies. Unfortunately, I was simply charged being African-American living in the suburbs. This was the start of my criminal history and first incarceration.

    email:20 Chapter:5. IN DIS CELL (MOST OF MY LIFE)"Mass incarceration tends to be categorized as a criminal justice issue as opposed to a racial justice or civil rights issue (or crisis)."-Michelle Alexander. The New Jim Crow Macomb County Juvenile Justice Center also so known as MCJJC. I can remember the first thing I felt once those steal doors closed me into a single man cell. I had been held in the Juvenile for Armed

IN DIS CELL DEANGELO ANTHONY

Robbery, and Home Invasion for the house that my friend and I stole the guns from the night of the alleged Robbery. The cell had a mat sitting atop a cement slab, and a cement desk along the wall. Cold air spewed from the air duct above the bed. There wasn't a toilet in these cells thus you had to hit a button and ask the staff member to allow you to use the restroom. Bathroom breaks were limited due to the fact a lot of the kids would manipulate themselves out of captivity. No one wanted to be locked in that cell by themselves. Mostly all of the children including myself had been heavily sedated with psychotropic medication. Sometimes ?kids would act out by beating on their cell doors or yelling to the top of their lungs. But I quickly learned that that only made things worse. I remember the first time out of my cell for breakfast. All the other kids had all been wearing prison clothes but we were able to keep our shoes. The smell of pancakes and sausage filled my nostrils while the staff passed our rations out. Some kids would trade off their food for their favorite items or the following meals. Surprisingly I wasn't the only black kids incarcerated there. There was kids from all over Detroit locked up in MCJJC for various crimes. One crime that was commonly issued out was car theft. The kids from Detroit found it better to come out to the suburban areas to boost vehicles. I didn't blame them because I've personally witnessed plenty vehicles with the cars running unattended. Most of the time we would play card games and watch television. We were allowed to go to gym and use the phone if you had good behavior. The staff really took a liking to me because I was very respectful and spoke with manners as my grandparents taught me growing up. My grandmother Naomi would always tell me to respect my elders. I would be able to get a few extra privileges such as staying up later than some of the kids or I would be able to go to the kitchen at night and eat a huge bowl of cereal. Sometimes we would hold Uker tournaments and the best team would get pop or chips if the staff felt generous enough to treat us for not making them work hard. Gym was like my favorite place to be because there was this staff member named Mr. Mark who had claimed to be Muhammad Ali body guard and he would train me to box. I had become obsessed with the sport. I never was able to really play sports such as basketball or football, I just wasn't into the game. Boxing was something that intrigued me because I learned it was more than just beating your opponent to the ground. It was like dancing and chess all wrapped up in one. You had to anticipate your opponent moves and be able to have footwork and most importantly be able to take a punch. I must admit that I wasn't too cool with getting punched so I had begun to practice on being a defensive fighter. Little did I know I would somewhat master the art of shoulder rolling, ducking and slipping punches.

      The first fight I had in juvenile was with this white kid who also had aspirations on being a boxer. We had got into it over the remote controller. The kid had seemed to always think that he could get me so one day I had finally had enough of his nonsense. His complex about black kids had grown deep in him as far as I knew. He would always brag about how he could beat black kids up and how he was stronger, bigger and that his brother beat multiple black kids up at some party. I never cared honestly, but It just irked my nerves to keep hearing him talk and it made me explode. I had called him out into the bathroom and we squared up. Both of us stood there as if we were in the ring and I just remember thinking that I would come out on top. However, I was wrong because soon as I had approached the kid he had jabbed me multiple times before I knew what hit me. I immediately reconsidered boxing and took it back to what I knew-all gloves off. I had eventually come out on top once I went back to the basics. My Master DE Angelo days had never failed me. That was the first time I had been restrained by staff members and placed on 'in cell' status. Going to court was always hard for me. I didn't like seeing how my mother looked at me standing before this referee or magistrate judge as I stood at the podium. I had this fat old white man that had reminded me of Santa Claus with this long whitebeard. He would seem to always hate to hear my voice. He never considered anything that I said and he would drill my mother into convincing me to take responsibility in something I didn't do. My mom would try her best not to cry or display weakness for me but I was always able to tell that she was dying inside. What Black mother wanted to see her son being railroaded into the system, same as his father? Every time it was time to leave at the end of the hearings she would shed tears watching as they escorted me back to the pods. Almost every time I had got back from court I would go in my cell and breakdown. I would make sure I cried with my face in the pillow because I never wanted the other kids to think I was weak or soft but I'm sure every kid cried after experiencing someone judging you and you not being able to go home to your family. I would push all my tears out and come out the cell with a chip on my shoulder. I was always mad at the world and the staff really felt bad for me because the kid that accused me for robbing him had been a repeated offender. Shane had been a misfit in deed. In fact it had turned out that I wasn't the only kid he had falsely accused for some crime. He had framed his own brother for something he didn't do. His brother name I do not recall but we've been on the same pod before during that time. He had told me that Shane was a heroin addict and had robbed their grandparents house to purchase drugs and called the authorities alleging his younger brother was observed carrying appliances out of their grandparents home. It was sad because his little brother had ended up having a rough time in juvenile. He had been allegedly raped by another kid in one of the showers. I remember trying to get Shane's little brother to tell his brother to tell the police the truth and that I wouldn't hold it against him. However, Shane had stuck to his story unapologetically. Days had turned into weeks, and weeks had turned into months. I had been away going on three months when the county had started constructing a new facility to house juvenile delinquents. A few kids had escaped during the construction of the building so we had been moved to another side of the old facility. I had witnessed other kids come and go to the point I became almost numb to being there. Most children didn't stay as long as I did unless you were fighting a serious crime such as Armed Robbery or Murder. Most of the other kids had petty crimes or were sex offenders. The sex offenders seemed to always get a slap on the wrist even when I became an adult. But the good thing about being moved to the other side we were able to see the females. I had found out that Tamara had been locked up there and we would be able to see them during our gym period in the halls. We would find little slick ways to pass notes or whatever. One of the only memories that had ran through my mind was the night Tamara and I had finally had sex. I sometimes think about her even to this day. The first time I saw her in the halls I instantly felt that longing for her. She cried soon as she seen me because she hadn't saw me since the night I was arrested. One of the staff Mr. Jordan had saw how we had interacted and one day let me get a few minutes to speak with her. Mr. Jordan was a cool staff member. We called him Mr. Jordan not simply because it was his actual last name, but he owned almost every pair of Jordan's back then. But me and Tamara had a quick embrace and I just remember hoping that we didn't move to the new building because I wouldn't be able to see her again. Sadly that was the last time I had ever seen or heard from Tamara again.

Chapter 5 IN DIS CELL (MOST OF MY LIFE)

It's like they had finished the new building just as I hoped they had never completed the construction. I was of the first group of male juvenile delinquents housed in the new units. This place was literally built and made exactly like a real cellblock. It had two galleries that had a huge cage on the second level to prevent kids from jumping over the rails. It had tables bolted to the floors with chess/checker patterns engraved on them. The cells had toilets and was setup exactly as prison cells. We had even been clothed in orange jumpsuits. I remember meeting this Latino kid that was from southwest Detroit and he would always act out and I'd act out with him? The staff started acting more like guards it was terrible. Instead of eating in the units we had been escorted to a huge chow hall. The male juvenile delinquents would sit on one side of the chow hall and the females would sit on the other side. We would walk through the chow lines getting our food placed on our plates they made it seem like we were actually in a real jail. That had really made a horrible impression on us. It made us start accepting the fact that we were prisoners. The new setting had started to wear on my mental. I had begun to experience deep depression and it was said that I would possibly be made to be a ward of the state if I was convicted of the Armed Robbery. I didn't understand what that meant for me and I had made my own conclusion to the status. I remember telling myself, IF MY MOTHER CANT HAVE ME

IN DIS CELL DEANGELO ANTHONY

NOBODY WILL. I just remember looking at the vent in my cell. I began to cry and think about all the time I had been locked up for a crime that I didn't commit and now they had been planning to make me a ward of the state. I thought being a state ward meant that I would be placed in some foster home or something where my family would never see me again until I was of age. Plus, I had been cool with one kid who had killed his little cousin and he had been charged with murder and he would tell me that that meant we would be locked up until we were 21 years old. The words of the detective started going through my head as well and I just collapsed to my knees in tears. I thought of my grandmother Arizona and how she'd always tell me to pray and ask God for the strength or plead the blood of Jesus, however that didn't work. I wanted out and there was no prayer that would open that door that night. So I ended up tying a sheet between the diamonds of the vent. I had tied the sheet around my neck and suddenly had a flashback of my little life. The eight months that I had been locked up in MCJJC had taken its toll and I remember jumping off the sink. I had been there choking to the point I think I passed out. I had this outer body experience or something I think. I had seen myself their hanging from the vent with foam and my eyes bulging from my head. There was this dark smoke rising from the corner of the cell floor and I remember my grandmother telling me that was the pits of hell opening up because if you were to ever commit suicide that was your one way ticket to hell. Before I knew it I was being cut down and taken to a mental house called Green Oaks somewhere far out in Macomb county. My mother had found out about it and was destroyed but happy that I hadn't been successful. To this day I would tell my mother that I wasn't serious and that I just knew I would get able to go to the mental house away from the Juvenile. But honestly, I really tried to end the pain that I was experiencing at such a young age and no child should have to go through such a thing. After nearly nine months of being incarcerated for a crime I didn't do, I had finally been given some relief. I had been strung out and forced to take a cobbs agreement. Even though I didn't do the Armed Robbery I still admitted to the crime because all I wanted to do was go home as far away from that facility as possible. I had been placed on probation for two years and was released to my mother.

Chapter 6 IN DIS CELL (MOST OF MY LIFE)

"The way out of trouble is never as simple as the way in."-Edgar Watson Howe. My family had relocated to Southfield Michigan to get away from East Point. I had been released on a two year probation where I had to report every month. I was drugged tested every month and would have to have no police contact nor truancy from school. It was like having a chain attached to my leg that retracted every time I thought about doing something wrong. At first I didn't even want to leave the house because going back to Juvenile was out the question, however at some point I allowed myself to enjoy my freedom recklessly. Psychologically that experience of being locked inside a cage and being away from my family for eight to nine months straight as a child was almost culture shocking. I would have nightmares about being back inside that godforsaken place. I even felt weird the first few months interacting with other kids my age. My mother had enrolled me at Oak Park High school. Oak Park High school was a decent school. There you had good teachers that actually wanted to teach you something. They had great sports programs and other curriculums like Mandarin class, Japanese class etc. High school at first was kind of hard for me as a freshman until my brother David started coaching me on things like how to get the ladies or how to dress. I didn't have all the designer but my brother made sure I was good in that department. He was a fashion guru. He had all the latest fashion and allowed me to wear his clothes to school as long as I didn't mess them up. I was horrible with shoes. I would always come back with scuffs or cresses in his Air Force Ones. He would hate that but he never neglected me. For the most part I attended school regularly. I actually did a fair job but it was just not the same after my juvenile experience. I felt I had to be this different individual. What I mean by that is I wanted to be that character that had been released from prison and he wants everybody to know that he was fresh out. That sort of made people fear me but they always wanted to hear about what it was like. Most of the kids that went to Oak Park really wasn't from the city. Thus, being able to be in the circumference of guys of my ilk made them look like they were of the same struggle. But honestly these guys had both parents in their homes. They had factory jobs and was fed with silver spoons. I had started hanging with the other kids that was actually from Detroit. We would fight all the other kids that was from eight mile or Southfield, Michigan. I had started getting very careless and I fell back into drug use. I smoked weed so much that my stepfather had to purchase me some Nicene pills so I could pass my drug test. Yeah, Rick ended up coming back around. My mother and him had still been good friends. In fact this Rick wasn't the villain he was when I was a kid. He ended up actually becoming very close to me. Rick had stayed at my mother's apartment until he got on his feet. So I'm going through all this nonsense in school and I'm doing drugs and one day me and Rick had sat down and we talked. I had told him that he really prepared me for the battles I would face unfortunately whether I wanted to endure them or not he made me a strong young man. I would sometime sell him weed and it was just a different Rick. I remember I was scheduled to go into my probation office and I was so scared that I would fail the drug test. Rick had prepared me this horrible remedy that was made of vinegar juice. I had to drink that with a gallon of water and I was using the bathroom left to right. However I ended up diluting my urine test. It was a passed analysis but my probation officer still violated me. It was absurd. After my first warning I was told not to use drugs but it was hard for me not to turn down drugs. Deep down I was dealing with so much pain and abandonment that I just found joy in smoking marijuana and hanging with my friends. I didn't even know how to be sober because that DE Angelo wasn't the guy everybody knew or liked. I wanted to be accepted and I thought that was the way to be cool and have people enjoying my company. With the continuation of doing drugs I started falling behind in my grades. I would go skip school with my homies and chill and smoke with the females. We would skip at my friends sister house or I would go to my stepbrother Jeremi house. My brother had lived with his uncle, grandmother and his girlfriend. I would chill with him and just basically say forget school. After a while Jeremi had ended up going to prison for setting a guy on fire and I started back dealing with my old friends. I remember one day during devils night there was this alternative school that was on nine mile. The football coach at Oak Park would always round up the kids that was skipping in his white Caprice and I happened to see his car in the lot at the other school. I had climbed the gate and set his car on fire. My father had also came back into my life. My brother David and I would go visit him. He had found a new girlfriend that took him in. I would go over their house and chill with my pops. His girlfriend Peaches had children of her own. I would embrace her and her children like they were my blood siblings. To this day we stay in touch and they been there for me as much as possible. But Peaches daughter Ashley at first I had this huge crush on her but she was so much like a sister to me that I stopped looking at her lustfully. Her little brother Jay land ended up being my little brother. I would teach him like that big brother he hadn't and because his older bro be beefing with all the other females in the neighborhood so I would be with her making sure she was straight. She would make sure I was good on all levels. We stayed high and drunk. My pops at that time accepted the fact that I had become my own man and instead of him being on my case he allowed me to do as I pleased. I had started selling burned CD's with my father. He was hustling all the latest movies and music. I had first figures out that I wanted to be a rapper when I was with him. I had listened to 50 Cent and G-Unit and thought like okay here's a guy that I could relate to in my time. 50 Cent was a true Gangster and I loved listening to him rap about his life experience and how he had did time growing up in South Jamaica Queens. I remember one of his bars that to this day I think about because he was serious when he said, YOU DON'T WANT ME TO BE YOUR KIDS ROLEMODEL/ILL SHOW EM HOW TO BUCK DEM THREE EIGHTIESAND LOAD UP DEM HOLLOWS/I just recall listening to that song smoking a blunt to myself

IN DIS CELL DEANGELO ANTHONY

playing with my chrome .380 pistol I had just gotten off one of Ashley's friends. I couldn't wait to get the opportunity to fire the weapon in the heat of battle. I didn't think about what the consequences would be if I had actually went out and used it on someone. I was always told that if you go out looking for trouble you'd surely find it. Well, one night I had found just that. It was a hot summer night and I was out and about with one of Ashley's friends. I had been selling weed and trying to live up to this tough guy persona. We had been driving around serving our marijuana and Ashley's friend had so happened to see a guy that had owed him some money. I remember thinking like YEAH HERE'S MY MOMENT. After following the guy around in his vehicle we had pulled up on one of the blocks he would hang on. Unbeknownst to the guy, so we thought, he didn't know we were trailing him. I pulled my little pistol out and checked the chamber like I'd see in the movies and I exited the vehicle. It's like the guy had known we were behind him because soon as I got out the passenger seat a hail of bullet store through the car we was in. Ashley friend quickly slammed on the gas pilling off as I fired back in the same direction the guy had been firing from. Ashley friend had pulled off and got nearly halfway up the block before he realized that I was still crouched behind a parked car exchanging fire with this guy. The block barely had houses on the block and you could tell that the only activities that took place on this block was drug deals and possibly murders so I was scared to death shooting this small caliber pistol looking for a way out of the situation. It was like an angel was with me because soon as I looked up to see if I could see exactly where the individual was that had me pinned behind the car, a bullet had struck the hood of the car I took cover behind. I could her screeching tires, and the smell of gunpowder heighten my awareness. Ashley friend had yelled my name as he reversed the vehicle toward the front of the car I took cover behind. I could see him ducked down reaching across the passenger seat to open the door. I dashed for the car as he floored the vehicle sideswiping several cars as we fishtailed off the block. After hitting several corners we had pulled over to assess ourselves. We both hadn't suffered any bullet wounds and later that night we had gotten word that the individual as well as, anyone else hadn't suffered any injuries neither. That was a close call and I was beyond blessed to make it out of that situation alive. I was only a kid and I couldn't imagine what that sort of lifestyle would bring until later in my story. This event had been the tipping point of my life because once I experienced this I thought I was really about that life then. I had went back to my mother's home in Southfield, Michigan with a new mentality. I had become a danger to myself as well as others. You would think after such near death experience I would change my life around but I wanted more, and more is what life began to throw at me. Troublesome like Tupac 96'. My brother had started to sense that I was getting into some deep things and he tried to intervene. He had introduced me to another way to express myself. Music was my brothers gift to me that had become a huge outlet for me to get things off my chest. I would listen to G-Unit and I adopted Young Buck as my favorite rapper. My brother would make me listen to Eminem and Jay-Z. He would point out punch lines and metaphors for me so I could understand the music from a more analytic way. I had found that poetry was extremely important to the format of music and my brother had purchased me a rhyming dictionary. I would put all kind of bars together and honestly it helped me say the things that I thought about doing instead of actually going out to do them. I had met my big homie Joker who had invited me to come chill at his apartment. He saw a bad little kid trying to be more than life offered and wanted to keep me out of trouble. He had been signed with Inter scope or something but his career had come to a halt and he started producing beats etc. One day he like get on the mic. So I had got on the mic and started to say whatever came to mind. This time I had been armed with more words for my vocabulary and my brother taught me techniques to flow better and I knew what I was saying. My first song ever recorded was at Jokers apartment and I remember taking it to my father and brother. They was like "yo' that's dope DE Angelo!" I had corrected them saying, "my rap name is Chaos!" They had laughed but was supportive like "okay chaos."

    My brother had started to sense that I was getting into some deep things and he tried to intervene. He had introduced me to another way to express myself. Music was my brothers gift to me that had become a huge outlet for me to get things off my chest. I would listen to G-Unit and I adopted Young Buck as my favorite rapper. My brother would make me listen to Eminem and Jay-Z. He would point out punch lines and metaphors for me so I could understand the music from a more analytic way. I had found that poetry was extremely important to the format of music and my brother had purchased me a rhyming dictionary. I would put all kind of bars together and honestly it helped me say the things that I thought about doing instead of actually going out to do them. I had met my big homie Joker who had invited me to come chill at his apartment. He saw a bad little kid trying to be more than life offered and wanted to keep me out of trouble. He had been signed with Inter scope or something but his career had come to a halt and he started producing beats etc. One day he like get on the mic. So I had got on the mic and started to say whatever came to mind. This time I had been armed with more words for my vocabulary and my brother taught me techniques to flow better and I knew what I was saying. My first song ever recorded was at Jokers apartment and I remember taking it to my father and brother. They was like "yo' that's dope DE Angelo!" I had corrected them saying, "my rap name is Chaos!" They had laughed but was supportive like "okay chaos. "My brother had started to work as a security guard at some place down town and at night he'd go perform shows with Ashley's older brother that owned a record label. My brother was the star on his label.

My Brother and One Down Productions had acquired quite the buzz and his career as a rapper started to look prominent. He had the baddest of the women. He had women from Canada that had hair that nearly dragged the floor. I envied him because I wanted to be just like my big brother David. His music I knew almost word for word. He would let me hear his new tracks and I'd be like "bro that's hard!" He was getting legitimate money working hard and investing in his music career until one day things took a huge turn for the worse. My brother had left for work one day with his head on his shoulders and next thing I know he had showed up at home not knowing his own name damn near. It was crazy. It was literally like he had lost his mind. Some jealous individual had laced my brothers weed being jealous of his position on their record label. My brother lost his entire life literally overnight; He lost his car; His job; His career and his mind all in one. I was so crushed because I had so much faith in my brother. He was my hero and some guy that he embraced as a friend laced his blunt and to this day my brother has never been the same. I couldn't even hold a conversation with him because I refused to accept this person he had become. It made me so sad and furious that it had drove me to more harder drugs. Depressed! I had started taking pain pills as if they would heal my hearts pain. Without that role model I had in my brother I sought brotherhood elsewhere to fill that void. I followed behind a bunch of losers and became one myself. I had gotten kicked out of school and my mother started to question what she should do for me. I stopped taking my mental health medication and I refused to go sit and speak to some stranger about my life's issues. Things had started to comeback full circle and my past had caught up with me. I dreaded the day I had to go report to my probation officer. I remember the long ride thinking WHY DID I LET MY MOTHER DRIVE ME OUT HERE? I knew I wasn't going to get out of this one. I had not been able to prepare for the drug test and I had all sorts of warrants for my arrest I just knew I had reached the end of the road but I had submitted willfully. I was tired and exhausted with my circumstances. After dropping dirty for marijuana, opioids and having several truancy warrants I had landed back in Macomb County Juvenile Justice Center. This time my stay would be a lot longer than the last time. I had been made a Ward of The State and sentenced to placement until I'd complete the program at a high security placement in Saginaw (Buena Vista),Michigan.

Chapter 7 IN DIS CELL (MOST OF MY LIFE)

"[T]he slave went free; stood a brief moment in the sun; then moved back again toward slavery."-W.E.B Du Bois, Black Reconstruction in America I had found this quote from W.E.B Du Bois in a book titled The New Jim Crow (Mass Incarceration in the Age of Colorblindness) by Michelle Alexander with anew forward by Dr. Cornel West. I felt that this quote fits perfect for this particular chapter because I was only out of juvenile a brief moment and I was being shipped out to a plantation like system. After spending a few months in the juvenile detention center I had been housed in Flint, Michigan at a juvenile facility called Genoese Valley Regional Center, where they housed all the high security status juvenile's. This place was like being in the county jail for real. It was a very old building and when I rode in they had made me cut my hair. I had braids at the time so I was pissed that they had made me get rid of my hair. I guess it was procedure. I was to be at this facility until a bed opened up for me at Wolverine Human Services to participate in their 18 month program if I did good time. Genoese Valley also known as GVRC was hard time. I remember the first time I had sat before all these other kids that was from predominantly Flint, Michigan. I had guys mean-mugging me like who was this kid from another city obviously. I had to introduce myself to the group and once I said where I was from I could immediately sense that guys hated kids from my city. One of the guys had looked at me and laughed and that was the first fight I had got in not even 24 hours being at this facility. I assumed that it would be like the prison movies where soon as you get tested or picked on by another inmate you was to immediately attack them so you won't be viewed as weak or victimized. Boy was that the wrong move. I had gotten jumped by like three other kids from Flint and they made it very clear that I wasn't welcomed. We had been on a strict schedule. You would get up for breakfast around 6am, lunch by 11am, and dinner by 4:30pm. While being at chow all the kids had to stand at the table and once everyone was in their personal stations we would be told to sit down. This chow hall was so small and the food was nasty as heck. I just remember wishing I was back home with my family. After chow we had to attend school. School was just another place I had to fight the kids from Flint. I would get jumped every other day until I had gotten cool with this one kid from Flint. My man's Love was in for a murder. He was not that much older than I and he was waiting for a bed at Maxi Boys Training. At gym the one kids I had been fighting with all the time tried to jump me and I just remember seeing Love toss a ball at one of the kids that was squaring up with me. The gym floors were so slippery and I was tussling with one kid trying to avoid being punched. These kids were way bigger than me because they had actual weights and I was this little guy that on paper seemed to be this hardcore criminal from Detroit. After seeing me fight nearly every other day, Love decided that I had enough and the other kids backed off. I would start working out with Love just sharing our little war story's. I found out that kids from Flint wasn't that much different than kids from Detroit. They had been faced with the same adversities. I was very intelligent then and I had been selected by one of the teachers to help other kids learn certain subjects. I wasn't too good at math but everything else I was passing with flying colors. We would also have to participate in group. Our groups consisted of various subject like substance abuse, anger management etc. If we paid attention and everybody added input or constructive criticism, the group staff would let us have leisure time. Leisure time we would be able to get board games or play card games or they would play movies for us. After about six months or so I had finally been transferred to Wolverine Human Services in Buena Vista. This facility was a high security placement that only housed about 80 kids. The place was secluded and a bulb wire gate ran along the perimeter. There was a huge football field and a small garden that could be seen from the parking lot. I remember walking through these blue doors and shivering from the cold air that blew throughout the facility. I had been taken to the annex building. I had seen the nurses and afterwards escorted to the unit I would spend majority of my time at. After a series of locked doors I had approached a huge gym. It was two full court basketball rims that was divided by this huge blue curtain that rolled back and forth. On one court there was a volleyball net at center court. On the far end of the gym you had a boxing ring, two pool tables, and two Ping-Pong tables. The housing units were divided into four pods that had side A or B. There was North A/B, South A/B, EastA/B, and West A/B. I was placed in East A. The pod housed thirteen kids and there was a classroom on the pod. We each had our own cells except for the first cell that was for a special status similar to a trustee called Victors. There was a lavatory on the pod that had showers, urinals and stalls in them. We were given a pair of black New Balances shoes, 7pairs of under wear/socks, 5 black shirts, 3 pair of black shorts and two sweat pants and shirts.

Each morning we had to make our beds military style. Corners folded with a 90 degree angle, our clothes would have to be rolled neatly into these little balls that I oddly still do today. We would come out and stand in front our doors and stand at attention. "ViewP.A's!!" one of the Victors would yell out to the other twelve kids for us to check our personal appearances. We would have to make sure our shirts are tucked in, our britches were above our waist and that our shoes were tied. "P.A's checked!!" we would reply after making sure we were appropriately dressed. Wolverine ran their program like a boot camp. We would have to walk in a single file line with our hands behind our back in the shape of a diamond and you were to always look forward and be a shoulder length apart from your peer. "Arm check!!" the Victor would say making sure we were not invading one another's personal space. Everywhere we went the Victor served as the group leader and he would lead us through the facility to chow, rec and outside activities. Being a Victor gave us special privileges. As a Victor you were able to enter the boxing program, pass outpoint store and be outside the unit nearly all day. We would attend school on our pods. We had this old lady who was our teacher. At first I would rebel in class until one day my teacher made a deal with me. I was very creative and loved doing arts and crafts. I would build model cars and create board games of my own to the point I had ended up being centerfold in the facilities News Magazine that circulated throughout all Wolverine Programming facilities over the state and abroad. I had created a human Chessboard and one day the Warden Mr. Wallik had offered me a scholarship to create a game that taught the juvenile kids the seven principles that was like the foundation for their reforming of us delinquents. The seven principles was Reality, Love, Education, Communication, Negotiation, Dedication... I'm not sure which one I left out but these affirmations sort of helped growing up. Mr. Wallik was an ex-convict. He had been a part of some organized crime ring similar to the Mafia in his younger days. He would come to the facility and interact with us in person. I would create all these decorations winning our unit holiday decoration events ever year and he would stop by and praise me for my creativity. I had become like this model inmate because my first six months I was just bad and I stayed fighting until I realized that if I do good time I'd get home sooner than I expected. I had earned all kind of certificates and was able to work in the kitchen. I was also able to join the boxing program and work with one of the coaches that had as on who was a pro boxer out of Saginaw. Things were not so bad until I had gotten into some trouble selling my medication to another kid. Once you got in trouble you'd have to basically restart the program. So I had to redo everything that I had accomplished which earned me another six months to make up my behavior. I had witnessed kids come and go. I had become one of like five kids that had been in the program. I had a eighteen month sentence so that six months pushed my date back. I had a few more setbacks which pushed my date back further and further. There was this motivational speaker that had come in to speak with us. He had been an ex-kingpin drug lord from California. I had been intrigued by his life story and I wanted to be just like him. He had changed his life and wrote books and would travel all over America talking to the troubled kids. He had once told me that all I have to do is educate myself and start putting my life into perspective. I sort of listened. I began writing my first book at the age of sixteen. I started reading a bunch of books. Two books that I had read that changed my mentality was The Rose That Grew Through Concrete by Tupac Shakur and The Prince by Niccolo Machiavelli. I got the book The Prince by a staff member who had it passed down through his father who had been a politician. The guy said that one day I would be great and I'd need that book as a tool to become a great leader. At that age I didn't understand what he was getting at but I read the book. Funny thing I still read that same book today. Well not the one he passed on to me but I ran across the book while being incarcerated in prison. My seventeenth birthday had been rapidly approaching and when you turned

IN DIS CELL DEANGELO ANTHONY

that age they would have to discharge you back into society. I had turned a 18 month program into almost two years but by the time I was supposed to be released I sort of had a new found attitude. I wanted to go to college, I wanted to be a writer and possibly a boxer. I wanted to be everything except another statistic. I was released After two successful home visits with no supervisions or worries in 2006. I was back out free as a bird.

Chapter 8 IN DIS CELL (MOST OF MY LIFE)

"Attitude Is The Way You Mentally Look At The World Around You. It Is How You View Your Environment And Your Future. It Is The Focus You Develop Toward Life Itself."-Selected I had done a total of almost four years in the juvenile system. I was now considered an adult and had the slightest ideal what that meant for me. I had been spit back into the community with very little experience as a young adult. My mother had found a home in Redford, Michigan. I had enrolled in the night schedule at Redford High school. Both my mother and father had once attended this school when they were younger. The little work/vocational education I had I was presented very few options to establish a career. Redford High school was a horrible school. I literally didn't learn a thing. This school was so bad that you could be in class sleep every day and pass with passing grades. The teachers were under paid and poorly equipped to render a proper education to the students. Plus, there was so much violence taking place around the school. I remember being in class and some kid was beefing with another group of kids and someone had fired shots into the classroom through one of the windows. It was crazy. My teacher was so cool. She would stop me before leaving class and ask could I sell her some weed. Even if I didn't have the product right then, she'd let me take an early lunch period so I can go to one of my guys in the neighborhood to grab her a few grams. I would do it because she always made sure I was good. Me and one of my guys from Joy Road was the only kids from our neighborhood that attended Redford. We didn't have to deal with all the nonsense taking place around us, thus we would hustle or chase the females. We thought we some kind of players. I personally never had an issue getting a female that I wanted. I was what I like to call a gentleman gangsta. I liked going on dates and spending quality time. All that romantic type stuff. Why? Because I enjoyed being able to not be this hard individual all the time. I wanted to relax and have fun. I tried to stay clean and out of trouble when I first got out. I went and applied for a job at this restaurant downtown Detroit by the Old Tigers stadium. Brooklyn Street Grill. I was hired on the spot because I applied the things I've learned while being in placement. I had earned a custodian maintenance certificate which helped me get the job creditability. Sadly that didn't last long. I refused to take the city bus to work and my mother wouldn't allow me to use her vehicle. I was supposed to show up for work that very next day and decided washing dishes wasn't for me. It was a very ignorant choice I made because they were willing to pay me good. After losing the job I was back at square one trying to figure out how I was going to make money. My mother had took me to get on social security, however, the few dollars I was getting wasn't enough to live one. Plus my mother would make me give her some of the money to help out with bills. Redford High school was on the list to be closed down, so I had to find another place to attend school. I just remember thinking like I'm just going to drop out and go for what I know but I didn't give up. Job Corps was an option I deeply considered. Me and my mother had went to register and I had ran into one of the counselors that once worked with me when I was a kid at Cooper Elementary on Detroit's Eastside. This lady remembered me instantly and made it her mission to get me in Job Corp. However, after looking into my juvenile records I was denied because they said I was convicted of a serious offense which was the Armed Robbery I was falsely accused of. I just couldn't catch a break so I broke down and returned to the streets. I started hanging with one of Ashley friends who was deep in the streets. It was a female. She was a butch and I would be with her every day. Ashley had introduced us before I went to juvenile the second time so she had an idea of what kind of guy I was. We would team up and hustle. One day her neighbor had did something and I just remember kicking in his door and brandishing this pistol I had. He was a big guy and the fact that he thought he was going to bully my home girl I wanted to make sure he knew we wasn't for any games. After firing Several shots into the ceiling he had started to offer me the content of his pockets and it was a wad of bills. I had taken the money and backed out the house and me and my home girl had went and got some drink, weed and pills all courtesy of him. That was the start of me realizing how easy it was to get money just by taking it. So I started robbing people. It's funny because here it was in my adolescents being framed for Armed Robbery to now actually doing Armed Robberies.

IN DIS CELL DEANGELO ANTHONY

This one particular event is what made me acknowledge that may be I was taking things too far. I was so far gone. I remember me and one of my guys from Joy Road had been way out in the suburbs visiting some females we had met after school. We were at this park just doing what teenagers do. I remember sitting at the mouth of the slide kissing this female and my sister friend Tracey kept calling my phone. She would let me get her pistol and I'd always keep it on me while I was out and about in case I ran across a lick. This day she had been roughed up by this guy and after calling several times I had decided to answer. I was so made because she had wanted me to come to her aid. I was just about to get to home base, but I immediately switched gears. We were so far out that there was no way to get to her in time. Thus, only option we had was to either steal a car or carjack one. I remember walking up on of the mile roads way out I saw a vehicle turning into a drive way heading for their garage. I made a B-line in the direction stealthily. I had been wearing all red sticking out like a sore thumb. I had approached the car gun pointed at the occupant. I had my brim covering my eyes as I spoke with authority. I demanded the person to give me the car keys and she wouldn't be harmed. The woman had spoken very calmly to me and what she had shared with me almost made my heart drop to my stomach. She said, "listen please don't hurt me. I'm a police officer in the Detroit area, my badge is in my glove compartment. My gun is there as well. "During this time 2007 it was a very bad year for police officers. They had been getting killed and ambushed all around the city of Detroit at the time. I just remember thinking that my friend really needed my help and I recall saying, "look my friend is in trouble and I need to get to her urgently. Now you can be another dead cop or you can give me the keys-your choice?" After I said what I said I could feel both of our energy change to a flight or fight moment. She had then replied, "look I have money in my wallet in the glove compartment, I'll give it to you but just please don't take my car it's all I have. I won't do anything crazy. "Mind you she had told me about her gun and badge being inside the compartment, I hesitated. I really didn't enjoy doing this woman like this because she was so calm and understood I was just a kid making a bad decision. I had allowed her to reach for the wallet to retrieve the money ignorantly. When I see the badge shining from the interior lights in her car I almost dropped my gun. She was smart though and I was too, she gave me the money and warned me if I ever came back near her home she would be sure to defend herself and her family. I ensured her that she would never see nor hear from me again as I backed out cautiously. I just remember me and my home boy running none stop trying to get as far away from the scene as possible. We were so scared and our adrenaline had been at its highest. Every time we heard a siren we ducked and dashed for cover. But to this day I'm thankful for that woman being so patient with me and helping me make the best decision for us both. If she would ever rear this in my book I would like to apologize sincerely for my actions and I hope she forgives me for what I done. In the midst of my life turning for the worse, I had ended up meeting my daughters mother Ciara. I had met my daughters mother through some mutual friends that I had made. My aunt Brenda's friend had introduced me to his nephews and I was later introduced to Ciara. Back then I never really appreciated the beauty of relationships in general. I had made a bet with one of the guys I met through my aunts friend that I would be able to lay her. After making good on my bet I had ended up catching feelings then one thing led to another. Learning that I had gotten Ciara pregnant was mind blowing. Here it was I could barely father myself, and now this girl was telling me that she was pregnant and I was the father. I didn't know the first thing about being a father. I never had one. Thus, I did whatever a 'boy' does when someone claims he's gotten them pregnant. I denied it. I denied it because I wasn't ready for those responsibilities. I enjoyed the sexual sensation but not that part. That added so much stress on me and I couldn't even take care of myself now there's a child in the picture? The news made me think that I had to be in a better financial position to take care of a child. I didn't know how to do anything else but crime. I knew if I did crime just long enough to acquire a certain amount of money I could invest it. Problem was I didn't have the slightest ideal what that investment looked like. One of my guys that I used to run with had been in the game. His family was big in the game and I would be with him a lot watching how things worked. He had a block he'd post on and make his sells. His clientele would come from all over the outer suburban areas like Dearborn, West Land etc. So I had asked my home boy to put me on. He was the kind a guy that really didn't believe in handouts plus he knew I didn't know too much about crack cocaine. My first put-on was a double up. A double is where whatever you put up currency wise you'd get double your money's worth. At first it was easy because I could just post on the block with my homie and once he'd run out of his product I would be able to make a few sells. The money that I was making always looked different than what my homie was making until he told me that he knew how to cook his product. One thing he didn't do was teach me how to turn soft powder cocaine into crack rock.

Joy Road around that time was a huge drug haven. It was so much money in the drug game that I started fantasizing about have all these expensive clothes, jewelry, the cars on rims etc. It was several young guys my age that was winning in that game. Thus, I wanted to get in the drug game. Selling weed was one thing, but dealing crack cocaine was a totally different ball game. One day I had went to the eastside to visit my family but I had brought my sack with me for safekeeping's. My mother was very noisy so that was the last thing I wanted her to find in her house. My uncle Bill lived somewhere off Gratiot and on that side of town there was a huge crack epidemic. I was my uncle Bills favorite nephew. My uncle Bill we called Blue. Uncle Blue was rich like three times out his life. He was a low key street guy but was smart enough to make legitimate investment's. His only downfall was his drug use. I remember sitting at his house with my little cousins and seeing how many drug addicts came to my uncles to either purchase product or share what they had. Once I saw that everybody came to my uncle, including the dealers, I knew that I would be able to work my way in and sell my product. I recall my uncle Bill digging in his pocket for the hard earned money he made middle maning for some dealer and at the same time handing it back over to feed his high. That's when I stepped up. I had told my uncle I found some drugs and maybe he could sell them so I can get me and my cousins some pizza. He had agreed and the sack I had sold out so quick that I needed more product. After coming back with more the next weekend that's when my uncle realized that my luck wasn't that great as it seemed. I was dealing and he knew it. Plus, I didn't know that users were able to nearly identify where the product came from. No one on his block Orin their neighborhood produced the quality product I had. I was getting my drugs from off the Westside and on the Westside guys used other things to cut their drugs verse what guys used on the eastside of town."DeAngelo where you get this from?" Uncle Blue had asked me. I was nervous because yeah I was old enough to make my own decisions but my uncles raised us up to be legitimate guys. Out all of my siblings I was the one that didn't do the sports or work regular nine to five jobs. I was a real street cat that had various resources that I learned to exploit. So I came clean, "Look unk I got my own plug and I need a place to roll my product because on the Westside it's too much competition. "That was all I needed to say. He had closed the door to the other dealers that had come to work his house and allowed me to set up shop. I still didn't know how to cook cocaine into crack and one day my uncle decided to teach me how to cook coke. I just remember standing over the stove with a hanger and a pirex scrapping, making all kind of noise as my uncle shouted instructions to me. All I could think about was how Young Jeezy glorified the dope game. It made me feel like i was cooking birds like The Snow Man. After messing up a few grams or so I had mastered the formula and now was able to advance in the business. What I didn't understand about the drug game was the severity of taking money out other people's pockets. You would've thought that my worries would been the authorities, however, they never even came on my uncles block. You can call them all day long they never cared. Somebody would literally have to be dead and the only reason they'd show up was because the EMS feared going in alone. I had recruited my cousin and we both took turns working the door. We would sit back smoking weed making sure our siblings had food and other things they needed. It would be a porcelain plate with a razor and precut stones waiting for someone to come by. I never had an issue making money that's for sure. However, I had a run in with a local dealer that had gota little serious. From that point I remember just purchasing every firearm I ran across. I had bulletproof vest all kind of protection to defend my turf. I had taught my cousins how to shoot the weapons the whole nine. After a while I started wanting to go back on my side of town. Summer time on Joy Road was the funniest. We had all the beautiful women etc. on the west so the longing for home plus the money started to mysteriously come up missing. My uncles that did the product would finesse me out my sack basically robbing me blind. On top of that my cousin was poor at saving the money. He almost always came back short. But one event is made me stop selling crack. I had despised the way my aunty Wanda was strung out. I would sell her the drug just to take the money and get food for my little cousins because they would be sitting there hungry without, so I called myself making a difference but realized I was actually doing the opposite. I saw how my little cousins looked at me when I handed their mother some drugs and she had already owed me some money... I see the look of fear in my cousins eyes because they had witnessed me react to people that owed me money. There it was I was letting her get deeper in my pockets and one day I had got very mad at her because I needed my money. In that game you couldn't be soft and you darn sure couldn't be a pushover and my family was the ones doing me wrong. So my thoughts of wanting to cause harm to my aunt was what made me say, "hey maybe I shouldn't be in this game?" That day I thought about making an example out of her, was the day I stopped selling crack completely. Well... Not completely!

CHAPTER 9 IN DIS CELL (MOST OF MY LIFE)

"Don't Think You're On The Right Road Just Because Its A Well-Beaten Path."-Author Unknown Towards the end of the year 2006, I had been back at square one. I quit the crack game and had no desire of getting back involved. The finances I did accumulate I had ran through and I was back on the block. Around this time I was still doing robberies and carjacking's. I would take on any mission that was available to get some money, especially now that I wasn't successful with the drug game. One of my guys had tried to direct me towards doing something different but I wasn't sold on the success rate. He like, "bro we can do music go get a deal and make it out like that." I had laughed because I'm like there wasn't a chance in hell we would have getting in the music industry. We did have the resources indeed. At one point the Street Lords was a huge group in the city of Detroit and we was tied in with Jessie James. Street Lord Jessie James was doing movies and videos all around our neighborhood and we'd be in the videos with the other kids from our neighborhood. It was an amazing experience for real because they made a lot of money making music and they would be driving all kind of cars and showing us love. So I knew we could get in the industry but we didn't even have a studio plug. The last person I had been associated with that had a booth I had fell out of contact with. I remember I had oddly acquired a music plug that had changed the trajectory of my life. True story! One day I was posted at one of the gas stations in my neighborhood. Our neighborhood was famous for this location due to it being a hot spot for crime. I was dressed in all black just posted with my guys from the block and this tile green bubble Capris had pulled up to one of the pumps. The sounds were slamming and it was a clean whip. You could hear the motor sounding like it was supped up. The occupant of the vehicle stumbled out the car staggering. He had been drunk as a skunk. I watched as he entered the gas station greeting the clerk and he pulled out a wad of cash. All I seen was twenties, fifties and hundred dollar bills in the palm of his hands. He had a pair of iced out Cartier frames on the brim of his nose. After a quick self talk I had formulated a plan to rob the guy for everything he had. I had this High Point nine millimeter glock. Having retrieved it from the chip rack where I hid it in case the police pulled up, I dashed pass the guy going to exit the gas station and he stopped me. He was heavyset and you could tell he was an older guy. I looked him in his eyes and it was like he knew I was up to something but he then said, "aye playboy where can I get some good from? Youwanna make some money? "You can imagine I was shocked and lost for words? He had paid the clerk and grabbed some Swisher Sweets from the slot. He asked me to follow him to his car. I followed him to the car thinking it would be easier to get him in his car. I just remember this beat blasting soon as I opened the passenger door. He had jumped in the car and turned the radio up even louder, then got out to pump his gas. Mind you I'm a total stranger that was plotting to rob this guy, but he wasn't scared at all which honestly made me very hesitant/nervous. I'm like this guy got to be nuts for trusting me thus far. The guy got back into his vehicle and asked me do I like the beat that was playing. I'm like yeah and he informed me that he did music and was looking for new talent. At first my mind was set on doing what I originally intended until he asked me to rap for him. I did and he loved my bars which was crazy because he wanted to sign me right there. Optimistic about his reaction he gave me his number and told me to contact him the next day so he could hear more. I had followed up and called the man to see if he was serious as I thought he was about my music. Turned out the guy was a man of his word. After talking to the sober version of the man who had seemed to remember ever bit of our conversation, he invited me to his house for further building. He lived right in the neighborhood. Walking distance. I met up with my home boy to tell him the news. At first he like"naw bro that's a setup he knew you was about to jack him..." I ignored his paranoia and went alone. When I got to the man's house he introduced me to his wife and children which made me feel very welcomed, and a lot more comfortable. Well his wife was mean as heck at first until I got to know her. He had some beats playing and I sat on the couch and started writing immediately. I knew that this was my chance to do what I loved doing and possibly get paid doing it. I wrote my first song almost on the spot. Listening carefully to every word I was saying, he like okay now we going to the studio. He didn't waste any time when it came to the music business. Music wasn't just my only option out of the circumstances, it was his as well as many others on his label. Big Tee aka T-Grymee was the CEO of Grymee Records. He introduced me to his producer Mell aka Melodic Beats and the rest was history. We would go on to record a compilation album and we performed all over the city. I had a show every day of the week no lie. I was doing shows on the Westside, east side and downtown Detroit.

T-Grymee was a well know guy. He grew up on Spokane and had ties on Schoolcraft. A true hustler hands down. He made money hand over fist. He had become like a father to me but I called him my uncle because my father was in my life at the time. May be not how I wanted him to be but he was there. But T-Grymee taught me everything I know. I was fashioned and groomed to be a real Hood Star. All the big homies he was connected to became family tome as well. I was like the kid in them Mafia movies that the family embraced. I'd get pinched and not run my mouth to the cops. They loved me because I was loyal and would listen to what they said unlike the other teenage kids in the neighborhood. I was introduced to a new kind of lifestyle. I was basically a local celebrity. We would pull up to the clubs fifty deep with a gang of women. Limousines packed with all the provisions you could name. We stayed drink the best. When I'd be with my other uncle who had joined the labels Management Team UncleKirk-Kirk aka Smit's we would be riding B.M.W's, Mercedes Benz the whole luxurious life I always wanted to live. Uncle Kirk was like a Dame Dash kind of guy. He was very in tuned to the music industry and at some point in his life he was a big time hustler doing whatever. He had did fed time and came home a mad man. Anyway, when he was younger he had made a song that some may be familiar with called 'Chips Ahoy' that had made BET. So he was a celebrity in his own right and most big time hitters knew him and had respect for him in the streets. Those two men became my role models and they never told me anything wrong. Anything I needed they would make sure I had it no matter what. They protected me and guided me down a path where if I hadn't gotten arrested on this case I'd been bigger than life. I was plugged with all the big time artist from Detroit at that time. Seven Da General, Street Lords Uncle Jessie James, J O'Neal etc. I performed with Stretch Money and my girlfriend Pam sister Billie was managing Royce Da '5 9. I use to be on Turbalance as well as, Video Vibe. Our Video came on every day and I had that recognition from the local music industry. Becoming this rapper I had to live up to my name. Young Cash from Grymee Records. I was acting anass. I would be in the clubs moving like I was the owner and guys would never say anything to me of the team that was around me. One night my bonhomie's had gotten tired of the way I was acting and staged a fade where this young cat that would be in our entourage had snuck me. I had gotten out my unlces Blue Beamer with my Marc Jacob goggles that I had just purchased. I was feeling myself and next thing I knew I was blindsided and had to stand on all the antics I had displayed when we were out. To me it was almost like an initiation because afterwards I was praised and saluted for holding my own. Even the relationship I had with uncle Kirk-Kirk and Big Tee had become stronger. I remember one day I was in my uncle Kirk Kirk red CL 500 Benz. We were having a discussion just the two of us. He was telling me how much potential I had and how I should take my career more serious. He had turned on my song 'I See You Haters' and told me to rap along with it. He stopped me when I was rapping because I didn't have the passion he was looking for so he like look. He pulled out stacks of cash with rubber bands wrapped around them, threw them in my lap and was like "now rap like you already got a million dollars". Now I got all this cash on my lap, I'm sitting in the driver's seat of this Benz with a well-known trap Star that I know made millions as well as, been in the music industry himself. I just remember that feeling I had driving that Benz through the neighborhood with my big homie in the passenger seat, rapping my song with me like we were shooting a video. From that day forth I wanted more and I knew exactly what I wanted to be. I wanted to be a Superstar Rapper. My dreams were on the horizon. We had just landed a distribution deal with Koch E-One Music. Salomon from P-Diddys 'Making The Band' had plugged us in with Choppa City Records. I had acquired my own resources with my peoples in Memphis that had linked me with Drum Squad. Drum Squad had invited me to come out to Atlanta. It was crazy how fast things had started to come to reality. During this time my daughter had been born and was so beautiful. I remember just crying with her on my chest while we were watching Cartoons. I just couldn't understand how I could make something so innocent and gorgeous as my daughter Myonna. She looked me in my eyes as I cried like she understood what was going on inside of me. I was battling myself because I had been exposed to all these luxurious things and in all actuality, I had not yet reached that point in my career where I was able to afford those kind of things. I wanted to create a life for my daughter and my family but I knew that I had a long way to go. With that being on my mind I had started living a double life. I would be performing at clubs across the city by night, selling drugs during the day and robbing during the break of dawn. It was crazy because I would still never meet the requirements I had in mind. It got so bad that my uncles would hear about some of the things I was doing in the streets and be like "Cash, you tripping just be patient." I wasn't trying to hear none of that. Here it was they exposed me to all this expensive stuff. They had the diamonds in their Cartier Glasses, they had stacks of cash and drove the finest cars and they told me to be patient? I had to get it but I would later admit that they were right...

Chapter 10 IN DIS CELL (MOST OF MY LIFE)

"Running With The Wrong Crowd Will Never Help You."-Ryan Cabrera Defiantly I had branched out from under the guidance of my Big homies T-Grymee and Uncle Kirk Kirk. I had been impatient and wanted to create my own way. I had linked up with some family from my sister Ashley side. Me and one of my guys had opened up our own trap house around the block from where my father had lived. I dated this female that had a house off Plymouth Road and we had agreed to help pay their bills while they allowed us to sell weed out their house. I didn't have to worry about any opposition due to the fact my father's girlfriend nephew had influence in the streets with the guys on that part of the neighborhood. Plus I didn't sell any of the drugs that would impede on their tuff. I was also taking trips out to Minnesota selling drugs out there. I was also running my own little operation down south in Memphis, Tennessee selling ecstasy and firearm's. I met this young intelligent female that I had instantly fell in love with. Lashell was my down chick. I would have the running things from Memphis, Tennessee to Detroit, Michigan. The fact that she was in the Army made it even better. She had also been a student at Mississippi University where we would go so she could do her ROTC training etc. It was the perfect match because she was all for me. I had met her at agas station one night me and my cousin Bae Bae had went to purchase some beers. I was connected with some guys once upon a time and we had a operation going in Canada. I would have my girl drive across the Ambassador Bridge with a careful of guns, and coming back with stacks of Canadian currency. We was making good money and it was a huge upgrade when it came to the things I was doing as far as hustling. I was not too far from being the plug myself. That was what every young kid my age wanted back then. We wanted to be the plug so we can get all the fame and glory from the streets. I was so trapped out thanks to Gucci and Young Jeezy. One day I had been setting up to prepare a rundown south with my peoples that way. I had been doing some last minute runs around the city and had stopped at my trap house on Plymouth. My girl had her friends over which I hated because I had an operation going there and that would compromise what I had going on. But this one day I just remember walking into the living room seeing this huge guy sitting there comfortably. I'm like WHO IS THIS CAT? I immediately pulled my girl and my home boy to the back room to question them. They were telling me that this guy was one of my girlfriends friend boyfriend. He had supposed to been looking for potential manpower to run an operation allegedly had going on somewhere deep east. I'm like I don't trust the guy and I'm cool just see if he could access some other things I was looking for to take on the road with me to Memphis. I had sat around with my girl listening to this guy talk. He had some outrageous story's that I honestly didn't believe. He was telling them all these story's that took place in the 80's and how he was this big time kingpin drug lord and he had a connect that he could link me with. I would blow him off every time he propositioned me. I remember him saying he was a part of an old drug ring from Detroit called the Best Friends. Now I was young and that was way before my time. I've heard of the crew running with Maseriti Rick and a few other legends. He had pulled up his shirt one day and showed us all his gun wounds. This guy had been shot everywhere you could catch a bullet. It's like he got shot everywhere but the bottom of his feet. It was crazy because there was No way he should have been alive to tell that story. He had started to tell us these war story's and how many people he killed etc. Now I'm like look, I ain't really interested in any of that. Anytime someone spoke on those sort of subjects I'd immediately exclude myself from the context. The night of me leaving for Memphis I had received call from my home girl telling me that she found something I was looking for. I rushed over to her house and picked her up. I remember stopping at my uncle's house first to let him know I was heading out. I had been dating this other female that turned out to be my sons mother. Kody was a wild girl but I love her because she was just like me but we complimented one another in our own way. We had an open relationship so I thought. I had been fighting with her all that week over my girlfriend that was from Memphis staying at my mother's house. I drove a white G6 and its me and my other home girl parked on my uncle block and I just remember sighing once I seen Kody sashaying down the block toward my car. She was instantly on me. It was like she was waiting for me to pull up on the block which I would normally do every day but I really wasn't supposed to be there this particular time. So Kody runs up to the car and jumps in the backseat. She starts trying to fight the other girl, questioning her. My home girl and I had never had any intimate relationship, she was just a friend. Kody was over reacting for nothing. We had fought her all the way up the block until I had wrecked my car trying to get away from her. It was like everything that day was trying to stop me from heading to Memphis.

    I had been able to drive the car back to my trap house on Plymouth so my father could assess the damage. The car wasn't totaled but it was not in shape to drive back to Memphis. After seeing that my vehicle was down, I ended up allowing my home girl to talk me into jumping in the car with this guy who was hanging around my trap house. He was supposed to been the plug for what I was looking for. So I'm mad at her because I had told her I didn't want to do business with this guy but she negated my hunch. I remember climbing in his forest green jeep. I had my home girl sit in the passenger seat, and I sat directly behind the man. Before heading to our destination, I recall us stopping at this house somewhere on the east side. The guy he met with was just so suspicious to me. It's like I could feel the energy was off. I couldn't place my finger on it. I hadn't been ignorant enough to come with some cash on my person, so I didn't think I was about to be robbed. I remember hearing him on his cellphone talking to somebody and he made sure I heard him say it was sixty thousand cash in his truck. That piqued my interest because it raised my suspension even more, but I couldn't show it. We had drove way out to Macomb on Thirteen Mile and Little Mack at this room. He convinced me to relax and told me just wait the person that had what I was trying to purchase would be there shortly. We in this hotel room with a few other guys, one of the guys was supposedly the guys nephew that I knew from juvenile. They offered to smoke until their runner had gotten back from wherever he had been. I obliged and as I'm rolling the blunt, I just remember nearly jumping out of my skin. The door had come crashing in. "DEA!! Freeze!!"the officers shouted as they breached the room guns pointed. They had cuffed us all up, sat us on the curb while they searched the room. I was so pissed because I wasn't even supposed to be there period. I remember the big guy telling me don't worry everything would be cool. I'm like what? He had to been blowing smoke up my rear when I heard the agents claim they confiscated over 500 grams of cocaine. My heart dropped when I walked into the Macomb County Jail. While we were waiting to get proceeded, I remember the police officers and the guy who I learned was Boone the notorious hit man for the Best Friends. Thing was he was a government informant. I had discovered they were already running a sting operation on his nephew and me and my home girl had been almost like bait. I just remember the way the officers excluded us from the context of their arrest. That alone made me think, DAMN, I KNEW IT! The way he spoke about old hits with the Macomb County Sheriff's was chilling because he was running around free as a bird. I had immediately shut my little operation down with my home girls and relocated elsewhere. I had later gotten news that same day I was released that the feds had intercepted my cousins down south. One of the connects I had in Detroit had got caught trafficking on the interstate on his way to Memphis behind my back. The connect ended up giving up everybody and my cousins where arrested and ended up serving fed time. I was relieved but mad the same time because my cousins were supposed to wait for me and allow me to handle all the business however, they moved ahead of me and got caught up doing it. I did feel bad though because I felt partly responsible. I had most of my funds wrapped up in that operation so it had hit my pockets pretty good to the point I didn't have that safety net I had accumulated. I was back at square one once again and this time it was worse because people known me for having a little money and being a hustler at that point. After the Memphis operation fell apart I had got with my father to get me a place to stay. My sons mother Kody was pregnant and needed somewhere to live. We had my father find us a house on Seven Mile. The house was nice as heck. Kodys mother helped us out with all the furniture and appliances. I had this huge Bull Massive living with us too. I had been doing good. One day after going through some other things in the streets my landlord had come to the house demanding to speak with my father. I had just gave my father a little over a thousand dollars to cover our rent etc. Kody had been almost nine months. Now this landlord begins to tell me that he never received any of the money I gave him. He and my father had made a special arrangement, that my father would fix on the house and we'd rent to own or something I didn't understand. Only thing I knew was I just gave my father my last to put a roof over my sons mother head while she was pregnant. The difference between Kody and my Daughters mother was Ciara was more responsible and had always kept food and shelter. Kody was always beefed out with her family, so she lived with me. Learning that my father had basically finessed me out of my money I had confronted him. One day me and Kody had come home to see his car in our driveway. I discovered him and my aunt in the bathroom doing whatever which infuriated me to the core. Kody also was livid. Her attitude was worse than minds. We both had been on the porch with my father and he had started to get loud and aggressive with my baby's mama Kody. Now I never seen my father get like that but he knew he was wrong for taking the little money we had when Kody was expecting any day. I just remember seeing him get all in Kody face and I lost it. I ran to my little 94' Escort and retrieved my Nine

Millimeter Carbine Rifle and before I knew it I was shooting at my own father. I never seen such fear in everybody's eyes and that's when

I think a few days after this event I went to get my SSI check from the mail box that was mailed to my father's residents the first of every month. He had been working on his car and once he seen me pull up I just remember him going to his porch. As I approached him trying to apologize for my actions, he had picked up a carjack and raised it above his head. He had threatened to bash it over my head if I took one more step. I knew he was serious as a heart attack and I didn't blame him. I had did the unforgivable. Regardless of what he had done I was never ever supposed to pull a weapon on my father. But I was young and dumb. I felt like I had to stand up to him because the way my baby mama looked at me when he was up in her face. However, she didn't agree with my response neither. In fact it scared her! Feeling ashamed and mentally disturbed I had started staying with another one of my big homies. He allowed me to live with him and his family. I would hustle and do whatever on his block. He did music too and he had introduced me to a few young guys my age. We would all do dirt together to make ends meet. I would be trying to hook up with my big homies girlfriend daughter Ashley. She was my baby. I was so into her but she seemed to not have that same feeling I had for me. But her and her friend Tyi had become my closest friends. I never had any sexual relationship or nothing with them. They were like my sisters. One day Ashley and I had been going to my mother's house out in Westland outside Detroit. I had this show lined up at one of the clubs I'd perform at. I had started inviting other talent such as my home boys that had a rap group called the Stack Boys. They were dope artist. Anyway, I had tried to sneak in my mother's house to get my clothes for the performance. However, Kody wasn't having that. She kept begging me to stay at home with her that night and once she seen me with Ashley she started to go off on me. So I'm tussling with my then pregnant child 'smother while she's swing on me and doing all that I sort of pushed her away to get in the car. I remember her and Ashley both turned on me. It was crazy because they were first arguing back and forth with each other to now both of them was on me. That night seemed to just be so weird. We had managed to get away from Kody but my mother had called me and told me to come home she had a dream that I had did something bad. I'm like man I'm not trying to hear none of that. I went out anyway. This promoter that I knew who had been promoting Grymee Records since we first started getting a buzz had met me at the front door of the club. He had informed me about how my single was being chopped and screwd down in Houston, Texas where he had just came from visiting. He had heard about me getting locked up and was like "Cash-Out! boy you stay in some mess boy. Stay out of trouble." I remember him telling me that it was a full house and that I would be called on stage towards the end. I had brought my guys with me to perform and showcase their talent but I expected to have performed and got that out the way so we could go on this mission we had. That night we had been put on a lick that was supposedly been worth our while. Knowing that and seeing that the promoter was trying to stall me out until later in the night to perform, I'm like "bro I got To go I got some money on the floor. "We ended up leaving the club before I could perform and next thing you know I was sitting in the Madison Heights Police Station waiting to be arraigned on Armed Robbery, Armed Robbery Conspiracy and Assault With Intent To Commit Murder. My actions had finally caught up with me and I would pay for the things I did whether I was innocent or guilty that particular time.

"If I Were Asked To Give What I Consider The Single Most Useful Bit Of Advice For All Humanity It Would Be This: Expect Trouble As An Inevitable Part Of Life And When It Comes, Hold Your Head High, Look It Squarely In The Eye And Say, 'I Will Be Bigger Than You. You Cannot Defeat Me.'"-Ann Landers July of 2009 I had been convicted for

IN DIS CELL DEANGELO ANTHONY

Armed Robbery and Armed Robbery conspiracy. I remember waiting to go in front of the judge. Before me it was this old man who had been a third habitual, first degree sex offender. When she had gave this man a ten year sentence I just swore up and down that my sentence would be a light one. However, I was wrong. For my first adult crime I was given a term to 20-40 years in the Michigan Department of Corrections. I was told that I would serve an amount of time that I hadn't even lived on this earth. I had just turned 20years old. My son Deandre had just been born and my daughter was two years old at the time. I hadn't been out of juvenile no longer than two and a half years which felt like a lifetime after all the things I had experienced. I remember being on this huge white bus that the inmates referred to as the Snow Bird. There was cages towards the front of the bus for high risk prisoners and the other prisoners would be shackled and chain around their belly's. The ride was a very uncomfortable and silent ride. You could tell that everybody on the bus was trying to mentally prepare themselves for what awaited us. Everything that I ever did in life had flashed before my eyes. It was as if I had died the way my life recapped. My emotions were null and void. I was literally numb. The smell of urine invaded my nostrils as I sat not too far in a seats towards the rear of the bus. My stomach ached. I had a migraine. The cuffs had been so tight on my wrist that the cold steel dug into my skin leaving an impression. As we traveled the beautiful but ugly, back roads of rural Michigan, all I could think about is how the heck was I going to do twenty years of my life in prison? I couldn't imagine what that would be like and

IN DIS CELL DEANGELO ANTHONY

I honestly wasn't ready for it. Whether ready or not, they sure were ready for me. After a long ride peering out the caged windows on the bus I remember having a conscious conversation with myself. I had asked God for a sign. I said, PLEASEGOD SHOW ME A SIGN THAT I'D BE OKAY? I had looked in the gloomy skies seeing hawks and Engle's flying around. So I asked God again, IF YOU WITH MESHOW ME ANOTHER EAGLE BEFORE I GET OFF THEBUS. I'm not sure if it was some miraculous event that was meant to answer my request, but sure as heck I saw an eagle just before pulling into the sally port at Jacksons RGC Facility. Looking back now, knowing the terrain where I was headed you'd see all sorts of wild life you wouldn't see living in the city of Detroit. The shuffle off the Snow Bird was the ultimate walk of shame. It was like everybody was watching. All eyes on us. Fresh fish as the inmates would say. Jackson Prison was a notorious prison back in my father days. I was sure I seen a ghost of the past lurking as these gates buzzed us in. The guards were shouting commands at us directing us to a seating area so they could take the chains off of us. I remember seeing this bulletin board in the bubble that marked every inmate that entered through the steel doors. At that time it had to be almost forty thousand prisoners that had come through Jackson either as permanent residents or temporary inmates. I was temporary if you would've asked me. In fact I'm sure every prisoner that came through them gates told themselves that they were temporary, even if they were sentenced to the duration of their life behind bars. Why? Because its two things that we were told before coming to prison. One, was you can beat your case on appeal. Two, they were bringing good-time back and you'd be able to get out early if you did goodtime. Unfortunately neither one would come for possibly 98 percent of those that walked through those gates. After seeing medical we had to go to the gym to get all of our state issued property. I could smell the paint that they used to number our clothing and the smell of new Oxford state shoes as if we walked into a Payless. There was so many young guys crowded in this gym. I mean it was packed from wall to wall with guys from all over the state of Michigan. It was oddly silent there as well. All you could hear was the voice of the officers instructing and directing the inmates around. Nothing but sad, depressed faces filled that gym. I sure was one of them! After getting our clothing we were escorted to our housing blocks were we would live until bed space was available at other facilities. I was amazed to see how high the galleries were as I entered 2 South. There was four galleries. You could barely extend your neck to see the top floor that's how high up cells were. My codefendant G-Man and I had been locking up on the backside on the forth gallery.

Chapter 11 IN DIS CELL (MOST OF MY LIFE)

Nothing can prepare you for that first night your in that single man cell in quarantine. Caged with nothing but your thoughts, and desires. All I could think about was how did I allow myself to be placed in a cage. I felt like some animal. My mind raced rapidly. I had experienced fear, anxiety and disappointment all at once. I would think about all the things I could've done. Didn't do, and what I'd do different when I 'Mable to walk out those doors. The guys that had already experienced their day one experience had knew that any talking after lights out was an excessive noise ticket and nobody wanted to be on Loss Of Privileges (LOP). There was this correction officer named Spiderman. Spiderman been around possibly since my father's first bid. He got his nickname because he'd literally scale the galleries to sneak up on prisoners for talking. He would just popup like, "that's an excessive noise!" He was notorious with the pen game. He enforced every rule. Then there was two other officers; James Brown was this older black officer that been around since the Jackson Prison days. He been working at the facility so long you could tease him from somewhere on the four gallery and he'd know exactly which cell your in from the front desk. I remember back then everybody would recite a joke that Mike Epps made about James Brown in one of his comedy stand ups, "get the light out of my face!" You'd hear another prisoner impersonate as the policeman that was arresting James Brown for his tax invasion case, "Why you run?!" Then Mike Epps would reply, "I ain't know whyy'all was chasing me! "But Robo Cop was a different breed. He was every stereotypical example you got in mind when it comes to a corrections officer. He was another legendary officer in the system. You'd wake up in the morning with ten tickets and be wondering what you'd done. He literally thought he was in the military or something. Your bed must be made, corners perfectly folded at ninety degree angle. You better have your I.d. Your shirt better be tucked in this guy was so petty. I think by time I left he had written me multiple misconducts. Showers was the worst part of prison. Especially at Jackson. There was an open shower pit and it would be a long line of prisoners waiting to get in. The officers would time you and believe you me, they counted every second. You had some guys who would try to shower fully naked. That was a no in prison. Only the homosexuals done things like that. If you'd showered naked predators would assume your propositioning them and that could turn out bad. I never had to worry about any of those things. I was already game tight because some of those same rules existed in juvenile as well. My first time on yard was life changing. You knew you were in prison when you hit that black top. All the prisoners would be in their respective circles. You would see orange hats everywhere winter, spring, summer or fall. It was either that orange hat or this blue ball cap. Everybody would be trying to work out getting ready for the gladiator school. Some guys peered off somewhere in space after being heavily medicated. Then those who may spend the rest of their lives there would be taunted by Cherry Hill which is the place they buried prisoners if they families didn't come get their bodies. One thing we all had to be aware of was the gun range that is in the vicinity of almost every prison to remind you if you cross that gate without permission they would not hesitate to shoot you. There was guards circling the perimeter in a pickup truck and guards hanging out gun towers with rifles. Most of my nights were like a bad dream. I remember staring out the rustic windows in this old ancient prison. I almost was able to imagine what the old yards looked like that my father once walk on with hundreds of men that did hardcore time. The empty basketball courts looked nearly inhabitable. The weeds grew through the cracks and the rims leaned as if they had been tired. I couldn't see my life being this prisoner. I had to come up with a better way to live. Get out of my situation unsaved. It was so hard to eat the food in the chow hall. There was so much going on. You had to watch your back and your front at the same time managing to eat all of your food. Most importantly you had to watch who you sat around due to their social status and or affiliation. I did most of my time around the guys that were from my city and especially my side of town. My first actual facility was Saginaw Correctional Facility. It was a total upgrade from where I had spent approximately ninety days or so. When I got to this facility it was arranged total different. You had a cellmate in this little cell with a bunk bed, a toilet/sink in the room with lockers on the wall. There was like these school desk where you'd set your appliances at or whatever you deemed worth displaying. I just remember carrying this green duffle bag with my state issued clothing with a blue wool bed roll tucked underneath my armpits. I sighed once I made it to my bunk after having traveled along way on in the caged blue minivan. Saginaw Correctional Facility was a wild prison back then. I wasn't there two days and witnessed a huge gang war take place. Guys were fist fighting on one end of the walk, two other inmates was stabbing another guy on the other end of the walk, while several others chased another guy towards the annex building. I was in awe. I just remember telling myself that I would have to prepare myself and be ready for war. I refused to be someone's victim.

    My first cellmate was this old school brother that was a student under the Nation Of Islam. I would sit back and watch him studying The Holy Bible and The Holy Quran all day. He would pray towards the east with his palms out speaking in the Arabic language sometimes. I didn't have a television so I had asked him to read a book and insisted that I read The Message To The Blackman by The Honorable Elijah Muhammad. At first I like man just give me an urban novel or an action novel. He didn't have any so I went ahead and read that book. The book was written simple to where I understood it, but the context challenged everything I was taught as a child under the Christian faith. But I kept an open mind. While the guys I knew from the streets would go to the basketball court or assassinate time, I found comfort in them legal books. I would go read up on the law and how to assist my appointed attorney with my appeal. I had learned how to shepardize and do research on cases. The black law dictionary was a book that I had to use a lot because a lot of the legal terminology I was illiterate to. There was so many books and court rules you'd have to sort through it was very overwhelming but I wanted my freedom. I had been seen by mental health and I was placed on outpatient Mental health status which prompted the administration to transfer me to a facility that had OPT. After being at Saginaw a few months I had been back on the Snow Bird but this time I was heading across the Mackinaw Bridge which was every prisoners fear because that's where you'd literally disappear. I was housed at Chippewa Correctional Facility but was transferred once again to Kinross Correctional Facility which was a level two. I had been lucky because you would normally have to serve seven years as a level four prisoner before you could get down to a level two. Due to the fact one of my codefendants were housed at Chippewa, I was moved. Kinross was an old military air base for the United States Air Force. There was five apartment units arranged in alphabetical order. This compound had housed at least 2500 hundred prisoners and during that particular time inmates could come and go as they pleased. We had keys to our rooms which capacity was four prisoners to one nice size room. We even had regular windows in our cells were you could climb in and out of if you wanted to. This place was wide open. There was two full basketball courts, two baseball diamonds, a back forty, a huge black top and the track ran at least a mile and a half in circumference. There was a gym with cubicles on two sides, a full court with hardwood floors and the school buildings were like walking to school from one unit to the building. This facility was huge! After you go through intake, you were automatically housed in the gym which was called G Block. Each cubicle had like six feet walls that provided each cube with some form of privacy. You had three cubbies that bunked in the cube. Two bunk beds per every pair of prisoners. There was card tables lined up with inmates playing poker or gambling on spades. There was pay phones on the back wall and I just remember seeing this guy arguing with his significant other about whatever. Another prisoner sat in a chair with his feet up on the phone as if he were at home somewhere. The noise level was unbearable. There was a lavatory and a day room they had a TV in it were prisoners piled up watching their programs. Walking out of the gym doors to the big yard was like being at an amusement park or a college campus. Or a scene from the kids movie sandlot. There was two teams playing their annual baseball game but the other team happened to be civilians from a local baseball team. There was spectators rooting for their respective favorite. I couldn't understand how they allowed prisoners to wield metal baseball bats hitting grand slams out the park. I started to walk the huge track alone trying to grasp the reality of things. My phone pin hadn't been activated and I hadn't yet ran into anyone I met. This compound was so large that the longer I walked passing tree lines where groups of inmates sat listening to their radios drinking spud juice. I could smell weed in the air. It was everything I anticipated this place to be. I ended up running into one of my guys from the world. My guy had been in prison possibly six months or so more than I had and he had already figured out the lay of the land. We walked around reminiscing about the good old days. As we neared the black top where

IN DIS CELL DEANGELO ANTHONY

hundreds of prisoners huddled in their respect groups we had been approached by two older gentlemen. "Young gods! How y'all brothers doing black men?" said one of the men. I had never been addressed as a 'young god' and I had reservations off bell because I didn't trust older prisoners due to the stigma you developed being ignorant to your environment. My home boy had greeted them with the Arabic words of peace, "Assalam-U- Alakim brothers!" The two gentlemen saluted us and preceded to speak with us. I had learned that these brothers were students of The Honorable Elijah Muhammad and his Black Muslims. They spoke very intelligently and made sure we understood their vernacular as they told us that we were the future and our people needs us to wake up and teach the people what had been stolen from them. 'The knowledge of Self' they called it. I had listened carefully and surprising I didn't get bored of it. After a little small talk but impacting, they had invited me to attend their Nation Of Islam classes.

Most of the stereotypes such as being approached by Black Muslims and using terms like 'black man', 'young god' or ' black queen' is definitely real. However, these experiences are part of the prison culture. Growing up I was indoctrinated under the apostolic faith so my ideal of God was Jesus Christ. I had encountered the 5%er Nation Gods & Earths when I was in the free world but I didn't have time to explore these foreign ideologies. I had met some of the Gods in D-Mecca before coming to prison, while living with my sister Ashley. I remember sitting on the front porch with my AK-47 propped up against the threshold of the front door. The seventy-five round banana clip poking out. I had a lap full of crack rocks on my lap counting a hand full of ones, five and ten dollar bills trying to impress this female. One the brother was visiting my sister cousin baby daddy whom also practiced the science, and out of nowhere the guy started telling me about the Supreme Mathematics and he broke down the days mathematics and how my street name Cash made me Self Sufficient which I was the given the attribute Self-Allah. I was intrigued and went to study with Dr. Bahu and the other Gods in D-Mecca but I had stop attending the meetings due to being distracted with the streets. However, my home boy had already been a believer in the teachings of the Nation Of Islam but I wasn't quite sold yet. I remember lying on my top bunk in tears silently speaking to God with the Bible open on my chest asking for guidance. See I had taken an entire different approach entering prison. I had immediately sought answers from a high being because I just didn't understand why my life had been so difficult. I would quote this poem that I had learned in juvenile reading Tupacs The Rose That Grew Through Concert. I'm not sure if its verbatim but here's how I said it; IF I FAILED TO ACHIEVE MY GOALSIF I STUMBLED AND CRUMBED AND LOSS MY SOULTHOSE WHO KNOW ME WOULD EASILY COSIGNTHERE'S NEVER BEEN A LIFE AS HARD AS MINDSNO FATHERNO MONEYNO CHANCENO GUIDEI ONLY FOLLOWED THE VOICE INSIDEIF IT

IN DIS CELL DEANGELO ANTHONY

LED ME THE WRONG WAY AND I DID NOT WINID TRY AND TRY TO ACHIEVE MY GOALS AGAIN I remember saying this poem over and over in my head because it was something that helped me navigate juvenile-however, prison was another beast. I had prayed and it was almost like something had spoken to me saying just read. It told me to go with the follow and trust the process which led me to signing up for the Protestant services. I wanted to see if what I was taught as a child was for me. I still remember walking into the service on a Sunday afternoon. I could hear the drums and organ playing familiar melodies as the double doors swung open. There was preaching and pulpit ting as you'd see in the world but something just wasn't right. I felt out of place and lost. I first thought maybe it was ?because I missed my grandmother and the family congregating on Sundays etc. However that wasn't the case. Something had told me to look around at my environment and I discovered exactly why I felt out of place and disconnected to the service. When I looked to my left there was groups of prisoners that I couldn't relate to. You had prisoners that practiced homosexuality. You had prisoners that had criminal sexual misconduct cases where they had allegedly molested children. You had side bar gang meetings taking place with multicultural groups. Please don't get me wrong, who am I to pass judgment on each particular lifestyle. The world as I knew it did not exist anymore and I understand that some people were born uncomfortable in their own skin and had their own sexual preference.

Also, some people are mentally disadvantaged and may have suffered some form of abuse in their childhood which may have made them believe it was okay to violate a young Innocent child. But... I do not personally agree with those kind of lifestyles but I can still view you as a human being with the right to live as you please as long as you are willing to live with your decisions. You are the Master of your own salvation. Thus, I had immediately signed off the Protestant services and gave The Nation Of Islam a try. I had been getting directed this direction since I was free. I never hadn't any knowledge of the context of their beliefs which piqued my interest because I wanted to learn. There was this man that I had encountered during my stay at Kinross that had claimed to grownup with my mother and father. At first I didn't believe him until he began to tell me things that only someone who had direct knowledge of would know. I remember asking my mother did she know this guy that claimed to grow up with her when she lived on Schoolcraft and I can't recall exactly her response but it was something that let me allow the man to occupy my time. He had been in the Nation Of Islamas well which to me was a sign. That made me say okay may be this is the direction God wants me to go. The first thing I had done was vowed to be open minded. I had fought with my old belief systems and at some point I had grown accustomed to learning about Religions. The Bible is by far the best book I've ever read. I am intrigued by the stories and history that it relates. The Bible became my first target because I've learned that it was the very tool that was used to manipulate the African Negro slaves almost five hundred years ago. They said the Africans had the land, and the Europeans had the Bible, being that our people were so spiritual, they offered to pray with us saying, "close your eyes and bow your heads." When the Africans opened their eyes they had the Bible and the Europeans had the land. It

I started from the beginning and discovered a huge contradiction in the story of Adam and Eve. Must I add, this is my favorite book in the Bible. The first thing that stood out to me was where it said "that God created man in his image and likeness." That was up for debate until where it read that God had said to someone else that they had become like us (Gods).And further it said let us protect the tree of life so that they may not live forever. (Genesis 1-3)Long story short, I had gotten very deep into the teachings of The Honorable Elijah Muhammad. I had earned my "X" exactly how Malcolm X did in his autobiography and I began to be very studious. At one point I had begun to feel as if I was not allowing myself to grow or experience my youth due to being ?so young in the system. I became robot like and also if you do not fully understand what you are learning regard to African American history, you'd find yourself being quite racist. That's not to say the NOI is a racist hate group. It's not the teachings it's the person that embodies the teaching without proper guidance, which expresses it in such manner. The Nation of Islam is very militant and move in a particular way. I needed the structure and the support but I still wanted to be a thug. Thus, I had went to my teacher and told them I wasn't ready to be so deep into the religion. Of course some brothers were disappointed in me, but they understood. I had been on this compound for like five or six months when I decided to find my own way. I continued to do my legal research and I had discovered a sentencing error and a few other issues that I researched and reported them to my appellant attorney. Once I was able to get my case submitted in the courts, I then focused on acquiring my education. I had passed the GED test with flying colors the first time taking it in 2010. So now I was educated and my legal affairs were pending. I had nothing left but time. Lots of it! I remember calling home every day just trying to stay connected to the world. However, one day my mother had answered her phone and posed a rhetorical question, "where you around the block or something?" she inquired. In my mind I'm thinking like WHAT IS THIS WOMAN TALKING ABOUT. I'M INPRISON DUH! But it had marinated on my brain and I understood exactly what she was saying. Calling home cost money and if you called every day, all day then you would see that you've spent a pretty penny. Plus, I'm sure she didn't want the constant reminder that her baby boy was in prison for twenty years. I sought other things to keep me busy. I had gotten a yard crew job where I made a mere seventeen cents a day. You'd work like a slave and at the end of the month during payroll your check would be like twenty-five dollars. I worked during the winter too so we had to shovel snow all kind

IN DIS CELL DEANGELO ANTHONY

things. Kinross did offer you a multitude of distractions outside from what the prisoners offered. With the inmates you'd see stabbings, fights and prison politics. The prison on the other hand was quite funny. They made sure you were comfortable like you were at some resort. They would take the waterholes during the winter and fill the courts with water to create an ice rink. They would also offer you skies and ice skates! I would do some cross country skiing one day and ice skate the next. But even that had gotten boring after a while. My first altercation had been with one of my cellmates. I had locked in a room with one of the Nation of Islam brothers that was from Los Angeles California. He had been this big homie from the Jungle's. I would be allowed to watch his TV or he would allow me to listen to Tupac on the Sony Cassette Player. He was so official. I remember we would be watching Training Day and he'd be pointing out all the members from the neighborhood he was from. We also had two other cellmates. My bunky was this older white guy. At first him and the brother formless Angeles bunk would get into arguments over common courtesy. The white guy would pass gas without warning and most of the time if I wasn't watching my big homie television, I would be on yard. However, I was confined to my cell serving Loss Of Privileges. The white guy rarely left the cell so it was just me and him in the room. I'm on my bunk and I just had happened to smell something fowl. I respectfully asked the man could he please step out the cell to do that. He flipped me off and then did it once again. I just remember taking this ink pen and I began stabbing him several times with it before it broke. The man had went to the corrections officer at the desk and told on me. They called me and inquiring about the situation and concluded that I was the aggressor and I was placed in segregation. Segregation at Kinross wasn't as bad because you had five other cellmates that would be in the room with you. So the whole time you playing card games, telling old stories and just passing time. I hadn't been given a serious assault so I did about thirty days in segregation for my first non-bondable misconduct. When I had gotten out of the hole I had been moved to another unity. I had some decent cellmates and one of the guys were from down south. He had sort of became like a big brother. He was a part of Larry Hoovers Chicago Organization and I would be with him and his guys. I would be drinking, smoking just jailing. I ended up collaborating with a guy I met from Saginaw and we were of the younger population. We would do everything we was doing in the streets. It was almost like I had too much freedom. After a while the things I was doing had been noticed and I had been found in possession of unauthorized medication used for whatever.

Chapter 12 IN DIS CELL (MOST OF MY LIFE)

"A Man's Errors Are His Portals Of Discovery."-James Joyce E.C Brooks Correctional Facility was my next facility. I had been place in the level four unit East Lake. Being at Brooks may been one of the most important times of my bid. I had sort of been lost and I needed to be in a more confined setting so that I may be able to limit my distractions. I had immediately settled into my new home. I had known several guys from the world that was also serving time there. That made it easier to get familiar with the terrain. Every facility you get to, the number one thing every prisoner should know is how the facility operates. You want to know the schedules? what officers be on nonsense? do we have any interaction with the lower level? who do I personally know? who running what? what groups control what? where are my respective group of individuals that have the same belief system as I do etc.? These things are vital to your survival because if you fail to have this in tell you are subject to move out of content and it can cost you severely. I've witnessed guys walk into these environments blind and nearly lose an eye or possibly their life. In prison there is always something lurking around the corner. You had to be vigilant and conscious at all times. Every yard has its own rules amongst inmates. Its own lingo. Things were so culturally different like being on some plantation. Even the choice of food would be signature; one prison might like steaming soups; one spot might do fried rice. But there are something's that are unspoken rules. You couldn't split guys on the walk ways, you couldn't use a particular phone unless you were affiliated with the individuals that claimed that phone, you couldn't sit at certain tables unless you were affiliated with this group or that group. You couldn't lock with homosexuals or someone would perceive you to be participant, you shouldn't gamble without having the funds on hand, you shouldn't borrow store goods unless you were able to pay your tabs and being a snitch was not tolerated. These rules applied to guys of my ilk. Everybody were not subjected to these rules. You had some guys that didn't live the lifestyle I chose to live in prison. Being a part of a Brotherhood such as The Nation Of Islam you have honor a certain code. Also a lot of those rules would actually keep you out of trouble and harm's way because each thing I've listed above came with consequences both administrative and amongst prisoners. Brooke's was what you called a Gladiator School. You had what they called the Milk Program that housed younger inmates so that they may attend educational programs. The Milk Program consisted of prisoners from the ages of 16-18 years old if I'm not mistaken. This brought a ton of violence. Add this with guys from every major city in Michigan you had a recipe for disaster. Being that I was around the age of my peers an being from Detroit, I moved with the guys from my city. We would do everything together. Work out, make cook ups and even fight other cities. In some cases you may have the surrounding cities like Pontiac or Ypsilanti or even Inkster that would merge with Detroit and we would fight with the tri-cities like Flint and Saginaw. Then you may have

IN DIS CELL DEANGELO ANTHONY

Bent Harbor, Grand Rapids, Kalamazoo and Battle Creek would merge with each other. With that being said you can image that there was a test of strength every day. A piss contest. You had to have heart because guys would try to punk you out. If you had fell victim to such you would basically be open season. Being open season meant you would get robbed. You would get assaulted and on some occasions you could get raped. Being at Brooks was the first time I had ever heard about a guy being raped. During my time at that facility two individuals had been raped and beat. Yeah, it was serious and if you weren't violent enough it could been you. When I had been in the vicinity of such behavior that's when I decided that I wanted to be the meanest, the toughest, the most gangster on the yard. I was already, and to this day, a smaller guy compared to some of these protein heads that lifted weights all day. But despite being small in stature, I was a big dog on the inside. I was ready for whatever and I've had my fair share of fights and stabbing during my prison bid. I had received good news from The Court of Appeals that my case had been remanded back to the circuit court. It was a huge chance that I would get a lighter sentence. All my research had paid off but my only worry was my prisoner record because I had acquired quite the reputation and when you have done so, your file would confirm your actions. I remember running to one of my guys from Joy Road telling him I was on my way home. He was happy for me as well as my other comrades. March of 2011 I had been remanded to the Oakland county jail on a writ for resentencing/reconsideration. My hopes were so high and I remember asking all the guys who were fresh off the streets about certain things that I wanted to get involved in. Honestly, my mind was far from prepared and mature enough to return to society at that time. I hate to say this, but I'm sure my judge had seen the same thing that I had confessed to myself deep down because when I went before her she had sat there with her glasses on the brim of her nose looking down at me from the podium once again. She had scanned over the documents that were before her and pausing for a brief second before allowing the prosecutor to state his motion for denial. He had been so compelling and made me out to be this villain once again

when he had finished his rebuttal I just dropped my head. The judge had denied my motion and reinstated my original sentence of twenty to forty years. I was a two time loser. That had affected me dearly. I just remember almost losing my hearing. It's like I was deaf and all I could see was her lips moving mouthing the same exact thing she said prior to my appeal. Crushed and destroyed I couldn't help but shed a few tears. I just wanted another chance at life but as I said I knew that I wasn't ready because otherwise I would've been resentenced. After spending about a month in the county jail I was so ready to get away from there. County time and prison time was drastically different. You were fed a little better. You had more things to occupy your time. You had more space to get away and the main thing that you wanted to get away from was the nagging jailbirds that cried about serving petty time in the county while kids like me were serving decades. I didn't even have space to think in that place. I was ready to go be a prisoner again. When I had made it back to Brooks I was mad at the world. I felt that I had been robbed out of an opportunity but I didn't realize that I was still the same individual I was that led me to prison. I remember the day I was sentenced and my daughters mother Pucci(rest her soul) had yelled to me as they were hauling me back to the holding tanks, "ain't nothing wrong with you boy! Don't change for nobody!" I'm not sure what DE Angelo she knew but I was very troublesome. My home girls Tyi and Ashley had come to visit me for moral support. They had been so excited to see me. Getting visits were the best incentive that any prisoner could have. It was so hard to get certain people approved such as my children. I wasn't able to see my children because I wasn't on their birth certificates. My children mothers were so consumed with themselves that they didn't think it was worth their time to track down these documents for me. I recall signing them when I was in the county jail but someone negated to turn them in to the secretary of state. I would beg my mother to bring my grandmother to see me but according to my aunts she was too old to travel such distance. I was approximately three hours away from Detroit. My siblings seemed to not want to see me so seeing Ashley and Tyi was amazing. I remember seeing my home girl Tyi have lustful eyes for me. It was like she seen this glow about me but we had never looked at one another in Such manner. Well, at least not me. Ashley, on the other hand, I had the biggest crush on. Okay, let me tell you a little more about this woman. When we were younger, she was what you would call a real trap queen. She was so game-tight and knew the streets better than most men.

I had gone to her one day with something that I didn't know how to put together, and she turned into this chemist on me. I watched in amazement as she did her thing. I was surprised but understood how she was so knowledgeable—she had been exactly like her mother. She came from that type of household, and she was what I always wanted in a woman. A trap queen! When you're serving time, you create this false perception that everybody is into you. A nurse could just greet a prisoner and he'd run to his guys like, "Yo, she on my tip," when she was simply being polite. We read into things because of that yearning for love.

I remember after a while, me and Ashley were building a lot. I had always tried to impress her. I remember talking like this ignorant nigga and she cut me off like, "Little D, you need to go read a book or something." I was so embarrassed. But I needed to hear that from her because it made me want to improve myself. I loved how outspoken she was. She never bit her tongue nor cared about your feelings.

I thought it was wise to cut into her one day, and she shot me down. It wasn't the fact that I couldn't accept rejection—I just couldn't accept it from her. That drew a huge wedge between us and we stopped communicating for a very long time.

After a while, I ran out of people to lean on in the world. My family almost instantaneously cut me off. I was destroyed because I had never done—

 Nothing but being the best brother, the best nephew, the best cousin, the best friend—and here I was, with no one there for me. I would lay my life down for anyone I loved. In fact, I came to prison on behalf of one of my big homies who told me his lights and gas were about to be cut off and he needed the cash to get back on his feet. I went on a mission for him. I didn't have to do any criminal activities, honestly.

My mother made sure we had everything we needed to be successful. I never actually went without. However, I was without on that yard. So, I turned to the family I had created on the prison yard. I needed cash and a way to obtain things like my appliances, etc., and one of my big homies provided a way for me to get on my feet. The big homies taught me how to figure things out for myself on the yard, and at some point, I decided to make my own moves. I acquired my own bag and started hustling on the yard.

Chapter 13 IN DIS CELL (MOST OF MY LIFE)

"When you speak, your words echo only across the room or down the hall. But when you write, your words echo down the ages." — Bud Gardner

The drug game wasn't much different than it was in the world. However someone got their product, it was still worth its weight in value. Inside, the market value was quadruple what it was on the street. I had started selling crack cocaine and heroin to other prisoners for Green Dots or Western Unions. I was making a few thousand here and there—but of course, the game had its downfalls. Outside of beefing with other competitors and dodging the drug hounds, you had to worry about snitches. I had let a guy get deep into my pockets, assuming he'd be able to cover his tab as usual. Little did I know, he had turned in a snitch kite. He gave up my full government name, my cell number, and even told the corrections officers that I didn't use or abuse any of the substances I had. One day, after making a sale, the very next morning at five o'clock sharp, the corrections officers came shaking down my cell. I was completely caught off guard and was found in possession of contraband. During my time in segregation at Brooks, awaiting my sentence after pleading out, me and a host of other inmates would play this game called "Shoot 'em Up – Bang! Bang!" It was a storyline game, kinda like Dungeons & Dragons, but with street narratives. We would be up all night playing this game. I had quite the imagination, as I mentioned before, which made me a great narrator. I'd paint these perfect scenarios with all kinds of twists and turns, and the other prisoners would walk through the world I created—verbally.

One day, we had been playing for so long we ended up sleeping through most of the day. But that night, I was exhausted and not really feeling up to playing. I remember one of my guys I looked up to from Southwest Detroit (Delray area) was in segregation with me after a big fight broke out between Saginaw and Detroit guys. He looked at me and said, "Lil bro, you be narrating some out-cold narratives. I think you should start writing books." I just remember being floored by that compliment—especially coming from one of the big homies. My guy was the real deal when it came to the street life. He was serving something like three natural life sentences for whatever. But I was like, damn, he's right. The fact that I was already good at expressing myself on paper, and had even written a book before back in juvenile, it just made sense. I immediately started writing my first urban fiction novel: Million Dollar Nightmares. Toward the end of March 2011, I was back on the bus—only this time I was headed to where the big boys go. I had finally made it to maximum security in just under three years. I remember pulling up to Ionia Maximum Security. Later, they would rename it Ionia Correctional Facility, as if that made any real difference. This place was everything my father had warned me about. It looked like the worst of the Department of Corrections was housed here. MI remember pulling into the sally port and being asked to recite my name and inmate number. I felt sick, honestly. I just knew I was going to be stuck in the maximum-security system for most of my prison term. Boy, did I predict my own demise. Maximum security was a Level 5 setting. Each prisoner had their own room. You were locked down 23-and-1—that's 23 hours a day, one hour out. You didn't even hear time the same way anymore. Everything was in military time. I remember asking an officer, "What time is it?"—trying to shuffle without scraping my ankles too badly from the shackles choking them—and he replied, "Thirteen hundred hours." I was like, what?!

After finally getting through intake, we were strip-searched. Here, there was no halfway doing what you were told. If they said "bend over, squat, and cough," you'd better just get it over with. Same routine everywhere, and honestly, I was numb to the motions by then. I remember the female deputy warden came to greet the new inmates. She laid it all out for us. The only thing I really heard from her long speech was: If you get into any trouble, I have no problem burying you in segregation. I was escorted across a quiet yard. All eyes were on me and the other new transfers from the Level 2 inmates working in the kitchen. Level 5 inmates were yelling out their windows. It was always like somebody was checking to see if they recognized anyone coming in. Real talk—prisoners are noisy. I walked into the segregation block where I was going to be housed, carrying my bedroll. Since I was in administrative segregation, I was still cuffed. You wouldn't believe how loud those units were. From the outside, it was dead quiet. But once you were inside, it was night and day. My ears were filled with madness—guys arguing, people yelling over each other, inmates "fishing" with bed strings and envelopes tied to them, gamblers shouting out point spreads and betting on the next sports event. Others were screaming at corrections officers for missing a roll of tissue or just for pissing them off. The only time that place went silent was when a female staff member—like a nurse—walked through. Guys would quiet down, waiting for her to get close just so they could expose themselves. It was like a zoo. It was crazy.

    The first time being in segregation at I-Max was hell. The first night there, I remember sitting at my desk trying to write in my novel when a weird smell seeped through my cell door. I instantly started coughing and gagging. The officers had performed a cell extraction and gassed one of the inmates. I dove beneath my wool blankets until the building aired out. The gas was so strong it would even go through the covers. You'd literally have to plug your nose and wrap shirts around your face and eyes. It was bad. Another thing I experienced was being lured to the door by an inmate to do what we call "selling slum. "Selling slum means roasting someone and putting all sorts of lies on their name. For example: One guy called me to the door during the late-night hours. I hadn't said anything to anyone since I'd gotten there. I finally broke the ice when I heard someone say, "Aye, ol' boy that just rode in!" I came to the door and acknowledged. The conversation started off with the usual random questions like: "Where you ride in from?" "What they call you?"

"You know so-and-so? "Why you in Level 5?" "Was it popping' off there? "Blah blah blah. After going through the motions and once the guy figured out enough information to build a fake narrative—here came the slum. So he acts like he'd been at a previous facility with me. And since I didn't expect him to be on some nonsense, I didn't question whether he really had been on another yard with me. The prison system is so small, you're bound to be at a facility with some of the same guys two or three times. So while I'm feeding into him, trying to extract some info myself, all of a sudden, he goes: "Nigga, you that nigga that was mess in' around with that boy on the back forty! You sissy!"Oh, did that set me off. I started calling the guy out his name, yelling over and over: "Where you know me from?! Where you know me from?! You can't know me!!!"This dude had me standing at the door for hours, cursing him out. After a while, when I started saying who I was, only then did someone I actually knew from a previous facility step up to the door. He called my name several times, but I didn't answer right away—still heated from what just happened. "Deangelo X!" When I heard him use my Muslim name, I knew he actually knew me. After some small talk, he told me the guy that was lying on my name had been in segregation for the past two years—on protective custody—for being a gang dropout and snitching on his own friends. I was relieved but still highly upset. I was glad someone cleared my name up, because like I said before, that was the last thing you'd want to be known for—especially back then. "A good name is better than silver and gold." It took me a few weeks before I could accept that I wasn't going anywhere anytime soon. My television finally arrived and I set my cell up. I had a schedule in place. I'd work out with my homie in the morning while watching BET videos until about ten. I'd take a bird bath, wait for chow to arrive at my door, eat, then take a nap until about two. After shift change, I'd sign up for showers or razors. Then I'd dedicate a couple hours to writing in my book until dinner. After dinner, I'd spend my leisure time playing chess with my neighbor, yelling numbers through the walls, or watching my TV programs. I remember one day I was sitting up writing in my book when I heard something that sounded like a waterfall above me. I turned off the TV that sat on my desk so I could hear better. Sitting there, segregation pen in hand, I felt drops of water hit my forehead. Man, I looked up and saw the ceiling leaking all kinds of water. I ran to the door and saw water falling over the gallery from above me. I ran back to the desk and huddled over my TV. Then I noticed my pages were getting wet. I snatched the TV's plug from the wall, threw it in the footlocker, then grabbed all my paper. By the time I secured everything I didn't want to get wet—I was drenched in toilet water. The guy above me hadn't gotten an item on his food tray, and since the officer didn't bring it to him, he decided to flood the rock by stuffing his toilet with bed sheets. One time, I witnessed two guys arguing through the cell doors. Mind you, we're in segregation. One guy yelled to the other: "You better have your strap, nigga!" I'm thinking: "OH—THEY ABOUT TO HAVE A KNIFE FIGHT." But then it hit me—it's physically impossible for them to even reach each other on the segregation yard. I'd heard about guys busting through the wall if they were neighbors, but these dudes were across the hall from each other. Turns out, at yard, they each had toothpaste containers filled with bodily fluids, and were squirting it at each other. These guys were so accurate, you could be in the middle of a full-blown shootout and still not get hit with the contents of their "straps." The gang culture at I-Max was thick. You had every gang and organization you could think of at that facility. The place was mostly dominated by Chicago factions, but there was a growing number of California sets that repped the color red.

One day, one of the guys I knew moved into the cell above me, after the officers finally got rid of the notorious toilet-flooder. I remember coming to the window—he had been in conversation with someone from the California lifestyle.

The guy had been from Inglewood, California. However he somehow ended up in the state of Michigan were he started teaching guys their culture. The guy had inquired if I had been involved in any of the cultural activities across the United States and I had related to this individual what I had experienced when I was a kid living in Memphis, Tennessee with students of Tookie Williams. I had never known too much about the other side but I thought we were just having a productive conversation. However, that wasn't the case for the young ignorant affiliates that assumed I was saying I was a part of the blue team. I remember standing on my bed looking out the window. The California guy had concluded our conversation with a question. He said, "you do know where you at right?" Unconsciously I had replied, "of course!" After going to sit back on my mat and going about my business, I pondered over the entire conversation and realized what he was asking me. I'm like "aww this guy must have taken what I said out of ?context." However, it was too late. Perception is reality. So now I had guys secretly thinking that I was active when I wasn't nowhere near that mind state. I just relayed my truth. I did associate with the other side unofficially. Right before the administration had decided to let me out of segregation I had received several kites. Guys were putting their bids in trying to build their respective teams up. I had no desire to be on none of that. I just wanted to do my time and get back to the lower levels. I had been housed in four block. When Ingot to the unit there was word shot out from my homie to his Chicago brothers. They identified themselves as Self, and I would be with them out on the yards. It didn't hit me at first that you could be guilty just by association. After being around them long enough, I started to pick up on their lingo and the little ways they carried themselves. My homie eventually got out of segregation and joined me in Four Block. We did our thing. I had become the housing unit barber, which gave me access to the entire unit. I'd be cutting hair and doing a little hustling or whatever. Me and my homie created our own little circle. We stayed in our own lane and handpicked the guys we wanted around us. Somehow, though, we ended up having a run-in with Self, which was odd. I guess there was a disagreement between two individuals that escalated. I didn't personally get caught up in it—but I still played a part, just by being involved. After that situation, the California sections started embracing us. We'd eat at chow with certain individuals from Inglewood who had UBN ties. There were so many different groups out of California that I didn't really know the difference—all I knew was they had strong unity. I loved how they showed brotherly love, but of course, there were always some in-house disputes. Some of the guys tried to get me to move with them under that lifestyle, but the fact that I was still free—free of anyone controlling how I did my bid—I didn't adopt the belief. Not yet. In April of 2012, I was transferred to another maximum-security prison: Marquette Branch Prison, way up north—across the swaying bridge, up in the mountains somewhere. I remember feeling so depressed when I saw it for the first time. This huge, old castle of a prison, literally built in the 1800s. You couldn't even see the yard until you passed through these massive golden gates behind a thirty-foot wall that wrapped around the entire compound.

Chapter 14 IN DIS CELL (MOST OF MY LIFE)

"You Have Enemies? Good. That Means You've Stood Up For Something, Sometime In Your Life."-Winston Churchill Marquette Branch Prison was a another story. I had to start an entire new chapter because I've spent so much of my term at this facility that I could be classified as a Upper. This place was were all the well known Gang leaders were housed. Instead of being behind cell doors you were in a bars setting similar to how it was in quarantine. I was housed in Golf Block. There was a total of two general population units and three segregation blocks. That's how much space they needed to house the inmates of Marquette because the prison would go up in to mayhem overnight. It didn't take much neither. Most of group warfare started over selling slum in segregation. Not to mention the other reasons such as gambling debts etc. Most of the time guys just popped off because they didn't want to be out on the yard during the coldest winters ever. I mean you would see snow piles four feet tall damn near all year around. Time at Marquette was a lot faster. You had way more things taking place around you. It was always something on the floor. You would be in your cell doing whatever you do and all of a sudden you'd hear the sound of a rifle going off. The corrections officer were armed in fully occupied gun towers. They had targets all over the prison where they'd fire warning shots. It look like San Quentin. I remember the first time I heard the rifle go off I nearly jumped out of my skin. By the time you leave Marquette Branch Prison for a lower level you damn near shell shocked. Real PTSD. A locker slam you think somebody fired a weapon. The first week at this prison I was in segregation for a fight. At some point I had been a repeated offender in segregation. The fact that I had a Major Mental Illness Disorder per federal law we could only be placed in segregation for up to seven days no bondable. Thus, I had become accustomed to putting in work. I didn't mind getting into any physical altercations because I would be right back out of segregation or the mental health treatment would refer me to a lower level of care i.e. Residential Treatment Program. I had got the attention of one of the top bosses on the yard. I had done a few things for some guys and one day I looked up there was several store bags at my cell door. Now there's a video they show you during orientation. In this video they warn you about the candy bar on the bed trick that the prisoners use to do back in the day to bait weaker inmates in to whatever weird games they had in mind. I personally haven't heard about anything of that nature in my time, but that's the first thing I thought about when I see all these bags at my cell door. Come to find out one of the situations I had handled everybody appreciated me removing a nuisance in the community. I remember the first time I met this individual. He had been in a circle of like twenty other guys from his neighborhood. There was a lot of Southwest Detroit guys at Marquette. I had been in a freestyle cipher with a few other guys and this individual had come over to listen to us rap. I had been rapping one of my best flows that I had recently written at the time. After I was done going he had approached me and complimented my lyrics. When I came to prison I literally left a show to go do something that resulted in me walking away from my dream. As talented as I was I didn't have the patience nor balls to make my own decisions. I had been a soldier loyal to my big homies. If I were told to jump I was dumb enough to ask how high? That was how blind my loyalty was. I was being misused and guys abused my loyalty. I was a pond on someone's board with the ideology that a pond would someday grow and become a king. So I didn't hesitate to put in work and that same dedication followed me to prison as well as, some of the things I had done to people in the streets. One day I had been building with my big homie while we were in segregation. I had sent my paperwork to him just to show that I was solid. I had my personal reasons why I wanted to validate my jacket. I remember the porter returning my paperwork and a few photos I had of some mutual individuals but what happened next was a huge reality check. I had found out that the victim of my case was the sibling of the platinum producer Helluva out the city. Like any ones loved one you would feel away if someone did something to your people right? Well I respected the code though I was young and ignorant of my choices I had been the only person that had to stand on my actions. By the time guys figured out I was involved in whatever I had been involved in I had already won over the love, loyalty and respect of this individual. In fact he had become like a father figure and role model to me. Even to this day we have that kind of bond. He taught me the ropes when it came to the groups festivities that took place around me.

IN DIS CELL DEANGELO ANTHONY

Around the end of 2012-13 I had decided to adopt the teachings of T-Rodgers. I had been introduced by a brother that was originally from West Los Angeles. I had begun living the lifestyle because I had loved the brotherly love. I wanted to fight for something greater than me. I needed something greater to fight for. Sadly my family and freedom wasn't enough because I couldn't see the end of the tunnel. I see what I had been subjected to and I had been consumed by the misery of it all. Twenty years of my life looked so far away and it was hard to accept reality. I needed a distraction. I needed moral support and I needed to be able to be me without all the religious restrictions and rules. I had five rules that I vowed to honor until my death and they were simple. Upon accepting this way of life I had to finally face my past. Remember the conversation I told you about with the Inglewood guy? Well someone had taken what I willfully exposed about my ties back in Memphis. This made it ten times harder to be seen as a legitimate brother. Though in the city where it originated from had such history of individuals crossing over for legitimate reasons whether they assumed it was about this or that but found out it wasn't. Even though I had not been a part of that honestly, I claimed it but perception is reality. With that being said I had to do ten times the work than the average individual. This caused me a lot of mental turmoil. I had been fighting to be accepted by my peers and at the same time every time I thought I had been a brother I would be betrayed due to political reasons. Guys would use this against me not because it really mattered. In all actuality it didn't matter whether if it were true or not because everybody came from something else they claimed to be loyal to. It was used only to discredit what I had over other individuals. The emotional part of it all had been almost unbearable. I had made a life choice and was locked into this decision because now that everybody said I couldn't be this, I wanted to prove them wrong. Opting out was out the question so I had to take the consequences. I would go on to blow my entire appeal for this false representation of brotherly love. I was possibly going to get ten years cut off of my sentence and I threw it away for some guys that didn't want nor respect me as their brother. I would defend the honor of some of these individuals and in return they would smear my name and plot against me. But I had memorized this Quranic verse that said, "men plot and plan but Allah is the best of Planners." I understood that no weapon formed against me shall prosper because I had a culling on my life that I would show up for regardless what anyone thought. The fear of not being accepted had evolved into audacity. It had turned in to boldness and I had been brave and consistent. But as I said this had bruised my mental because I had real love for what I had begun to live. I loved it and everything in it as if it was my own flesh and blood. Loyal to a fault. I remember being in segregation talking to my mother about her decision to leave Michigan. When she told me that there was nothing here for her I broke down inside. She said , "I can't even come visit you because you wanted to sell drugs in there. You always doing something!"...To this day it's been thirteen years since I last hugged my mother. I had failed her because every time I went out on that yard trying to prove my loyalty to something that wasn't loyal to me, I would not be able to get my visiting privileges back. I was under a two year policy where every ticket that you acquired would reset your two year clock. Even though I hadn't even been found or accused for smuggling on a visit my family had been found guilty by the state as well. If a prison get caught with some fermented orange juice he would lose his visiting privileges. If it happen twice it will be indefinite. This is how they do us. Our families are punished for something that had nothing to do with them period. It's the same way when it came to restitution or court fees. Every penny my family would send me the state would take everything over ten dollars as if my family was paying the debt to society as well. I remember being in segregation and I just had had enough. I wanted out of this oppressive state and attempted to commit suicide once again. I had consumed a hundred Tylenol tablets. After several hours thinking it would be enough to do the job I had quickly realized that this wasn't what I wanted. I wasn't ready to give up. I still had fight in me. Even after witnessing multiple suicides happen I just didn't want to be weak. So I sought help. I had been sent to the hospital and put on IVs. They had to flush my system of the substance. After spending a day or so in the Marquette General Hospital I had been returned to the facility and placed on suicide watch. I had been so ashamed sitting in the bare cell naked wearing a thick bam bam gown. I didn't have the desire to eat or talk to anyone. I was deeply depressed and despite not wanting to end my life I was still questionable. I had been dealt a bad hand and it's always been because of my loyalty to everything and everybody but MYSELF! I had become my own worst enemy...

Chapter 15 IN DIS CELL (MOST OF MY LIFE)

"You Cannot Decide When Or Where You Will Die, But You Can Decide How You Will Live."-Selected After being placed in acute care to accommodate my severe mental disorder, I had been shipped out of Woodlawn Correctional Facility to Gus Harrison Correctional facility. The treatment had got me a waiver to the lower level to participate in the Residential Treatment Program. I had been placed on Secure Status which was a step program. In SSRTP you would have to do up to a month confined to a single man cell with limited movement. There was groups that you were to attend during the morning where they would shackle and place you in belly chains like Hannibal Lectern or some psychopath. The mental health team was very hands on. You would participate in multiple classes but most of the time you would watch movies. After group you'd get a chance to shower and that would be your whole day. Being on the secure status also prohibited you from having any property i.e. appliances, paperwork, stationary or miscellaneous items. You were only able to have your under clothing and two orange jumpsuits. It took me a few days before I decided to start interacting with others. Most of the individuals were so mentally incompetent that I was way out of place. Word had gotten out that I had rode into the program and I had got a window call by some individuals that lived the lifestyle. I remember thinking like MAN I'M NOT IN THERIGHT HEAD SPACE, however, when I did look out to the yard in the neighboring housing unit I saw that it was one of the guys who had been beefing with the United front I had moved with. He had been in the program as well. He had a few other young homies with him and they had wanted to make sure we didn't carry the beefs from the max to the program. Everybody in the program wasn't suffering some sort of mental breakdown. Most of the time guys would manipulate the program to get a break from all the nonsense that took place in the maximum security prisons. I had agreed to a cease fire sort of speak on behalf of the circumstances. Plus I wasn't even thinking about this guy period. I had been trying to gain myself-esteem back after attempting suicide. Plus I had been trying to situate my legal work. After being denied when I went back for remand, I had been preparing my Motion For Relief in the Michigan Supreme Courts. The clock had been reaching ahead. I had been approved for the legal writer program but due to the fact I had been on secure status and couldn't obtain my legal work, Marquette Branch Prison failed to forward my legal file. My appeal had been returned to me with the rubberstamp saying that I had exceeded the statute of limitations. The courts went on to tell me that there was no exception for the tolling of time. DENIED! After getting the news about my court proceedings I been bombarded with bad news. My aunt Ernestine had passed away as well as, my big homie T-Grymee wife had died as well. I needed to get out of this emotional ditch I seemed to keep digging. I found going to the window talking to one of the young homies from the life that had always wanted to build with me about our history. Adkeyda "Lil Mook" Boyd had been this young dog from the Westside. He had just came to prison and transferred in from Macomb Correctional facility. We would just build and he'd put me up on the latest trends and fashion that was going on in the world. It had been five years since I had last been on the streets. I found talking to the younger homies helped keep you relevant and updated on life that you had known. Lil Mook was a this wild young dog. He had been in the Inglewood household and on the strength of that I took to him. I had grown knowledgeable of their history and outside of that Lil Mook was just this cool dude. I would have him contact my mother for me because I couldn't get to the phone due to my status. He had been beefed out with the Correctional Officers in his housing unit. I would allow him to vent and then render him sound advice. He would always look to me to talk him off the ledge almost. I remember I had been written a phone restriction because the officers that he was at odds with would check his call logs to see if he used any unauthorized pin numbers. I wasn't mad at him though the phone was vital for me being that my family didn't live in the state. I remember just observing this young brother swaging on the yard swinging his dead arm that had been disabled after being shot in the world by the police or somebody. He would be so loud and obnoxious rapping his music. I knew then exactly why he had some of the troubles he had with the officers. He was what they feared most. A young black male with no fear in him. He had been suicidal, homicidal all wrapped in being a part of one of the most violent street gangs in the MDOC. Most of the guys of my ilk that had started representing was wild and violent. We didn't have any elders to guide us because it was a young pack that had just got footing here in Michigan. The older homies that had been around turned out to be bogus.

Lexus Nexus had dethroned/exposed all the old heads that would claim they had this big homie status. It was so many guys that had ran the system that turned out to be bogus. It had destroyed every group in our state because with the exposure of these leaders it had left a huge void. You had the blind leading the blind and we had to rebuild our way with what he saw fit for our state. Thus, you had a spike in independent sets forming all over the state. After getting the news about my big homie from West Los Angeles, I had nearly wanted to become a civilian. I had a bad experience with doing things for guys that turned out to be someone other than whom they claimed to be. But I still had a pride issue and I had been so deep into the lifestyle that I even feared walking away because of the many adversaries that would be like vultures waiting on me to get weak. I had banded with another brother and we united with a concept that made us responsible for our own destiny. The few guys that we did educate on what we were doing had been handpicked by either myself or the other individual. I had met this young brother that had claimed ties to the neighborhood I'm from. He had been Related Thru Money and being that I personally knew some of the kids he ran with I embraced him. He had been fighting a federal indictment for whatever they accused them kids of. All I knew of was he passed the inspection on the state level so I let him move with me. I had become bunk mates with the guy that had been opposition to the faction I dealt with prior in the max. Due to him being the person that presented the information on my ex-big homie we had buried the hatched and summed it up as water under the bridge. After making it on the next phase of the SSRTP program I had been able to get out my cell more. I had got a job and the Correctional officers would allow me to come out porter and do my little dirt under their noses. I think they had felt bad for me because sadly the young brother Lil Mook told you about had committed suicide. Yeah, I remember that like it was yesterday...Before progressing to the next phase in the program, I had been up with Lil Mook all night for his 21st birthday. April 21, 2014. I would make jokes about how we couldn't even buy liquor as if the legal age wasn't twenty one. I just demonstrated the same love the big homies had shared with me when I turned twenty-one in prison. We talked out the window all night drunk off spud juice. That following day after his birthday he had come to my window complaining about how the officers kept pressing his bid. He seemed really disturbed but not suicidal. I had been dealing with my own issues. The administration had been on to me and was looking into my associations, plus I still hadn't gotten over my problems. I just remember him repeating,"Fxxk this I'm about to shoot my move." Shooting a move means a prisoner acting like he would harm himself to manipulate his diagnosis. The Mental Health Team would almost always come to your aid and bail you out of trouble. I had gotten tired of him complaining every day and I just remember telling him, "bro my kids at home. Iain's no niggas father you a grown man do what you do." That was the worse advise I could've ever given the kid because literally thirty minutes later guys were yelling across the yard saying he had been found hanging from a sheet in his cell. To this very day I feel responsible because if I'd just pushed a little hard an been a tad bit more patient with him he'd possibly be alive today. I had been called out by Internal Affairs because I had been over heard on the phone talking with Lil Mook mother. She had been told he had just didn't want to live and he killed himself when that wasn't the case. He had been beefing with these officers and instead of them going to his aid as it states in the suicide prevention protocols, they knew he was trying to manipulate the system. They passed by his cell and that was that. But his mother was not that much older than me. She was from the neighborhood too and I couldn't allow her son to be smeared in his death. They assassinated his character and I had to make up for not being the responsible brother. When Lil Mook passed I wanted revenge. I felt that the administration had been responsible and I wanted to make them stand on that. Conflicted over what I could do to acquire justice on his behalf, I had suppressed my emotions and vow to get back. I learned that all Correctional officers were not the enemy. In fact I had gained the respect for the few that had come to work and did their job. A lot of officers brought their personal life to work and took it out on us.

Luckily the officers I had been around saw that I needed something to take my mind off my homie death. I had caught the eye of a female staff that had seemed to be obsessed with me. She would always compliment my locks and say I reminded her of MillieVanilli. I had the slightest idea who the heck that was but later I learned it was a music group in the 90'smade famous for lip singing. This woman would be so obvious about her desires and I would be trying to tell her like, "yo' your fronting us off. Tighten up." It was like she didn't care about her job.

   We would establish a secret relationship beyond the means of her job description. My peers began to notice us interacting during our groups and like most of these dudes, they tried to backdoor me and blackmail her. She would tell me that the young guy I had brought on my team, Don D, who had been awaiting his trial with the feds on the RTM indictment would be threatening to tell the authorities about us. Shocked but not really convinced that the kid would play me like that. However, despite what I personally wanted to believe, the kid had wrote a snitch kite to the administration alleging that me and another prisoner were overheard plotting to beat and rape several female staff members. This was a serious allegation and a for sure ride out. I had been taken to segregation and told about the allegations. It had been so unbelievable that I laughed and felt like I was in an episode of Punk'd or Prank Wars. But it wasn't a joke. It was real and now I was accused of planning something that I had never did. I didn't even believe in such violation of any female period. I had more respect for them and myself. I despised that sort of offense because my father had once upon of time violated my favorite cousins when they were young girls and that was why he had been absent in my childhood. Deep down I never forgave him for this nor had I ever inquired to either him or my two female cousins about what actually happened. Thus, I had spiraled once again. This mental breakdown was not even six months since the last attempt that I made on my life. I found myself in observation again after trying to harm myself. I couldn't live with that on my name. Not only because of my father but having those kind of cases in prison automatically made you bold. Plus I didn't want my daughter or my mother or my sister to even assume something like that ever crossed my mind. I was in Adrian Mississippi. They called Gus Harrison Correctional facility Adrian Mississippi because they were known to operate as if they were still in Jim Crow south, thus, in their eyes I was guilty. However, after being transferred back to Marquette Branch Prison on an emergency ride out I had been found not guilty of the misconduct. The findings were that I could not have done what was alleged due to the date and time of where this plot was supposedly overheard. I was framed and written a false misconduct and punished for it. That event was the tipping of the iceberg and what compelled me to start my fight against the injustice in the penal system. I had filed a 1983 civil claim with the help of a jailhouse lawyer and immediately proceeded to get relief for the violation of my constitutional rights. The few us prisoners have thereof.

Chapter 16 IN DIS CELL (MOST OF MY LIFE)

"Do Not Follow Where The Path May Lead. Go, Instead, Where There Is No Path And Leave A Trail."-Ralph Waldo Emerson2015 I had been back at Marquette Branch Prison. Even after being away for a little under seven months it was like I'd never left. It was still things going on that was going on when I had last been there. Brother on Brother violence was at an all-time high. It was almost like a purge had been taken place. Unfortunately, my name had been on that list. I had spoken with a young brother that I had personally educated that pushed the agenda against me. There was a huge campaign on me behind ones assumption, however, I never folded under pressure. I had stood on everything that I had believed in. I believed in brotherly love overriding oppression and destruction in society. It was the only thing that inspired me to keep fighting. I had been released on the compound and it was said that I was under a no fly zone with my brothers. I had went out on the yard the first day out and confronted several alleged conspirators. After approaching these guys without a lick of fear I had instantly earned a new found respect for who I became. I was a Kamikaze pilot little did they know. After being in an altercation with an individual, I was back in segregation. During my segregation term I had ran back into one of my guys from the neighborhood. Capone Da Capo was a young charismatic individual that had been aspiring to establish his own publishing company. However, despite such ambition he lacked the material to actually publish. Plus, most of the individuals that claimed they were aspiring authors had not even completed their drafts. Me on the other hand, I had been almost four complete manuscripts in. Of course it took some pointers from one of the old heads. Larsen Bey was a magnificent writer. He had been in segregation for escaping maximum security way back when, and he'd be the brother that would be encouraging the youth to strive to be better. I had been one of the guys he had deemed worthy of his time and assistance. I had been penning Million Dollar Nightmares and he had literally taught me the proper way to write a manuscript. At first I would just write line for line. My sentencing structure and punctuation was terrible. I had to basically go back and literally learn how to write. It had been sometime since I had passed my GED test. I had passed writing with a 720! But here it was I didn't know how to write correctly. Thus, Larsen Bey had helped me learn how to better my writing. I would read several books on the craft and he'd have me sending him chapters and if they were not done right he'd mark them and send them back for me to revise them. It took me literally three years to write my first urban novel and I had written it a total of eight times. Capone Da Capo had inquired to review some of my work. Me and the homie had history and at one point I defended his honor awhile back. He had instantly fell in love with the story. He had been more fortunate than most and had propositioned on a partnership agreement. He'd put up the finances and I'd put up Million Dollar Nightmares. In my eyes it was equal partnership. At first I had desired to get a publishing deal with an established publishing house. I would write letters on top of letters to submissions. I had inquired to Teri Woods and she had wrote me a personal letter and sent an autographed flier only after I wrote and sent her greetings cards literally for like four Christmas's, wishing her a happy holiday. At one point she had told me that she had some legal trouble and she wasn't accepting manuscripts at that time. I still shouted her out every year though. I even went as far as making collages out magazine cut outs for cover design ideas. I was serious about what I wanted to accomplish. I remember the homies would make fun of me in segregation when I'd ask them for all the old magazines. One homie was like, "what you doing making a third grade project?" He had all the other homies laughing at me. I can't lie I even laughed but I wasn't laughing with them I was laughing at them and they would soon see that everything I had done led up to this ultimate victory. November of 2015 I had self-published. Million Dollar Nightmares was available on all platforms. We had been the first of our generation of prisoners to accomplish this. We even beat the guys that taught us the game at it. One of the big homies Harbin Bey had plugged me with Avid Readers Publication. He had wanted to see me win and he saw I was serious about what I wanted. He was another legend out of Chicago. I had also ran into one of my guys that I had been doing segregation time with. He had been partly responsible for me adopting the lifestyle. He had been in segregation when I had come back for an attempt to smuggle. It's like soon as I started doing something positive the administration had sought to dismantle our progress. I would get so many

IN DIS CELL DEANGELO ANTHONY

Notice Of Intent claiming that I was running a business and that it was gang related all sorts of sabotage. I was making some real power moves and they took notice of it. I would be talking to Big Meech wife one day asking could she forward him a copy of my book. The next day I'd be talking to an elementary school teacher about a kids book I was writing. I even had a guy out New York my brother plugged me with that wanted to make a movie script out of my book. Or they'd hear me instructing my friends and family on what to do. They hated that. This one sergeant had come to my cell side and told me to stop preaching! Honest to God Truth.

"Do Not Follow Where The Path May Lead. Go, Instead, Where There Is No Path And Leave A Trail."-Ralph Waldo Emerson2015 I had been back at Marquette Branch Prison. Even after being away for a little under seven months it was like I'd never left. It was still things going on that was going on when I had last been there. Brother on Brother violence was at an all-time high. It was almost like a purge had been taken place. Unfortunately, my name had been on that list. I had spoken with a young brother that I had personally educated that pushed the agenda against me. There was a huge campaign on me behind ones assumption, however, I never folded under pressure. I had stood on everything that I had believed in. I believed in brotherly love overriding oppression and destruction in society. It was the only thing that inspired me to keep fighting. I had been released on the compound and it was said that I was under a no fly zone with my brothers. I had went out on the yard the first day out and confronted several alleged conspirators. After approaching these guys without a lick of fear I had instantly earned a new found respect for who I became. I was a Kamikaze pilot little did they know. After being in an altercation with an individual, I was back in segregation. During my segregation term I had ran back into one of my guys from the neighborhood. Capone Da Capo was a young charismatic individual that had been aspiring to establish his own publishing company. However, despite such ambition he lacked the material to actually publish. Plus, most of the individuals that claimed they were aspiring authors had not even completed their drafts. Me on the other hand, I had been almost four complete manuscripts in. Of course it took some pointers from one of the old heads. Larsen Bey was a magnificent writer. He had been in segregation for escaping maximum security way back when, and he'd be the brother that would be encouraging the youth to strive to be better. I had been one of the guys he had deemed worthy of his time and assistance. I had been penning Million Dollar Nightmares and he had literally taught me the proper way to write a manuscript. At first I would just write line for line. My sentencing structure and punctuation was terrible. I had to basically go back and literally learn how to write. It had been sometime since I had passed my GED test. I had passed writing with a 720! But here it was I didn't know how to write correctly. Thus, Larsen Bey had helped me learn how to better my writing. I would read several books on the craft and he'd have me sending him chapters and if they were not done right he'd mark them and send them back for me to revise them. It took me literally three years to write my first urban novel and I had written it a total of eight times. Capone Da Capo had inquired to review some of my work. Me and the homie had history and at one point I defended his honor awhile back. He had instantly fell in love with the story. He had been more fortunate than most and had propositioned on a partnership agreement. He'd put up the finances and I'd put up Million Dollar Nightmares. In my eyes it was equal partnership. At first I had desired to get a publishing deal with an established publishing house. I would write letters on top of letters to submissions. I had inquired to Teri Woods and she had wrote me a personal letter and sent an autographed flier only after I wrote and sent her greetings cards literally for like four Christmas's, wishing her a happy holiday. At one point she had told me that she had some legal trouble and she wasn't accepting manuscripts at that time. I still shouted her out every year though. I even went as far as making collages out magazine cut outs for cover design ideas. I was serious about what I wanted to accomplish. I remember the homies would make fun of me in segregation when I'd ask them for all the old magazines. One homie was like, "what you doing making a third grade project?" He had all the other homies laughing at me. I can't lie I even laughed but I wasn't laughing with them I was laughing at them and they would soon see that everything I had done led up to this ultimate victory. November of 2015 I had self-published. Million Dollar Nightmares was available on all platforms. We had been the first of our generation of prisoners to accomplish this. We even beat the guys that taught us the game at it. One of the big homies Harbin Bey had plugged me with Avid Readers Publication. He had wanted to see me win and he saw I was serious about what I wanted. He was another legend out of Chicago. I had also ran into one of my guys that I had been doing segregation time with. He had been partly responsible for me adopting the lifestyle. He had been in segregation when I had come back for an attempt to smuggle. It's like soon as I started doing something positive the administration had sought to dismantle our progress. I would get so many Notice Of Intent claiming that I was running a business and that it was gang related all sorts of sabotage. I was making some real power moves and they took notice of it. I would be talking to Big Meech wife one day asking could she forward him a copy of my book. The next day I'd be talking to an elementary school teacher about a kids book I was writing. I even had a guy out New York my brother plugged me with that wanted to make a movie script out of my book. Or they'd hear me instructing my friends and family on what to do. They hated that. This one sergeant had come to my cell side and told me to stop preaching! Honest to God Truth.

    I would be soapboxing to my peers about how we should use our time to accomplish real moves. I had acquired all kinds of financial literacy like Rich Dad Poor Dad serious by Robert Kyioski. I would read The Art Of War by both Sun Tzu and Niccolo Machiavelli. Robert Greens 48 Laws of Power.50 Cents 50th Law etc. I just really started to blossom into a highly intelligent being. I knew that I had to make a contribution to myself, my family and my brotherhood. This is what made me the biggest threat to my captors. Anyhow, I had decided to unite with a new strong breed of Dogs. My birthday became May 25th, 2011. I would go on to fully embrace the embodiment of being that Bad Guy. I wanted to be with guys of my ilk and genuinely build as a band of brothers for a worthy cause.

Chapter 17 IN DIS CELL (MOST OF MY LIFE)

"A Good Head And A Good Heart Are Always A Formidable Combination."-Nelson Mandela My brothers had finally deemed me worthy of being honored. I had withstood the test of time and now it was time for me to progress beyond the maximum security prisons. I had been transferred to Brooks once again. I had earned my visitation privileges back after eight years of restrictions. I was excited to get closer to the city so I could finally see my family and friends. I had started rekindling a lot of my relationships. I had hardened my heart and became so numb to the point I had nearly cut everybody off. I wanted to fix that and that's exactly what I started to do. I had gotten back in my children's life. I made sure I did as much as I can for them and stayed relevant in their minds. They had still been babies then so I would talk to them but I didn't quite think it was the right time to start holding deep conversation with them. But I made sure they knew exactly who I was. I had been reaching out to my siblings. I sent visitation applications out to everybody. My uncle Bill and my home girl Tyi had been the only ones to complete the forms. I had been anticipating a visit from Tyi. It had been so long since I've last seen her. It was 2018, the last time I saw her was in 2010. I remember going to get my Locks twisted and my lineup an tapper. I had been building with her on the phone for a few days. She had just gotten out an abusive relationship and finally had been free to live without worry. She had just been hired at the plant and got her a little house somewhere in the city. She was doing great and she was ready to be back in my life. I remember being so anxious. The weekend was approaching and I was to see her that Saturday. I had begun calling to make sure our date was still as planned. However, I would get no answer. It went all the way until the day she was supposed to come see me. I had not been able to reach her and due to my past trauma I assumed she had stood me up. Crushed and mad at her I had not been able to get that visit. I remember talking to my mother having her call her phone numerous of times and my mother like, "boy you keep calling her she might have a boyfriend. Stop bugging that girl." I just didn't feel right about it because Tyi was a solid female and a true friend tome. She would never just ghost me like that. If she couldn't make it she had no problem saying 'aye I can't make it. 'Sure show my hunch had been correct. Ashley had popped back up in my life and been the barer of bad news. I had learned that she had been found naked with bullet wounds to the face and chest area. Her niece had been in the hospital fighting for her life after their assailant had come to execute them both. I dropped the phone because she didn't deserve what happened to her. There was all kind of allegations of who people thought or assumed did it....Man that was a hard story to tell you. Her death still pains me because I felt that if I would've not been in here getting into all this mess may be I would've had my visitation privileges and been able to see her and hug her before her life had been ended so early. She was still young and had so much potential. She had been robbed of that but that was an event that made me reflect back on my actions. I had never knew what it felt like to have someone you loved taken away from you or harmed in a violent way. I told myself that I would never do harm to my people unless I had to defend myself, my family and my beliefs. To be honest that vow I made didn't last a week. I had been deep in prison politics which resulted in me being rode out on an emergency transfer. I had been placed on the suspect list for my ties to my Guys. It was alleged that I had something to do with a ranking officer being stabbed at Marquette Branch Prison. The administration wanted to STG me but they seemed to be able to keep me still long enough to do so. I had been sent to Carson City which was an upgrade tome.2019 was an amazing year for me. I had been able to get my life in order there. I lived like I was a freeman. I'm wearing Cartier glasses and Air Max 95's. I was back up to my old tricks and I had been around for quite some time which provided me a lot of resources. I remember I had this young guy as my bunk mate. Lil Goose was from Pontiac, Michigan. We jailed great together. He knew how to do his time and move on the yards. He had always use to be writing music and he had inspired me to start back writing music. I would use writing music as an outlet to express myself. It was life changing to be able to get all these things off my chest. I would rap about my painful experiences with being a product of my environment. Sometimes I'd just write bars talking about nothing but I made it sound good.

One day Lil Goose had introduced me to one of his bros. The guy had heard me rapping out the door. Most of the time we'd be rapping and beating on the doors on our down time. He had approached me like, "bro you think you can ghostwrite for somebody?" I had reflected on what he inquired and was like, "I can do whatever!" Come to find out he had been trying to get me to ghostwrite for his baby mama. Now that was a challenge. Being the person I am I wanted see if I could actually do it. Besides I was writing all these songs with the slightest ideal of how I would be able to record them. So I started writing music for his baby mama. However, it was all trap music and I hadn't even spoke with her to grasp the kind of artist she was.

When I was at Carson City Correctional facility, one of my guys and his guys had obtained a phone. They had decided to go live on Facebook doing they thing. The video had ended up going viral. It had made the news. They called it, THE CARSON CITY BLOCK PARTY. It was funny as heck. I just remember saying to myself, MAN IMMA SHOOT A REAL MUSIC VIDEO. Mind you this 2019. It was just a thought. I had only spoke with one person about this idea. Lil Goose was like, "bro you crazy. How you going to do that?" I really didn't know I was just running my mouth. I had got into a group fight with some guys in the chow hall and I had been placed on another emergency transfer.

This time I was back across the bridge at one of the worse facilities in the state. Chippewa Correctional Facility aka URF'ed. I remember the first day I hit the compound. I had been fresh as you could ever be in prison. I'm rocking my Cartier's with the big 55" lens. My yellow and black Air Max 95's had been complimented with a yellow and black fitted jacket that I had purchased at that facility. I mean I thought I was the fourth Migo or something. Homies like bro you look like you about to go to a video shoot. I can't lie I loved walking through them yards with my head high looking like a bag of money. However, these officers were a different breed. They were openly racist. At Earth they would call you the N word in your face and dare you to do something. I remember the sergeant had dashed out of the guard shack like, "hey guy!! Yeah you!" At first I'm like man I'm not about to even acknowledge this dude. I know he on nonsense. However, that was a unnecessary ticket that I wasn't willing to catch. He had started questioning me asking am I a part of some Latin group because of the colors etc. I'm like "I'm not a part of nothing sir." He had told me, "look you at URF now and we don't play that here. If I see you come out like that again I'm coming to take your shoes etc. "I had come right in testing their patience. I remember running back into the brother I told you about that was like a father figure to me that I encountered while serving time at Marquette Branch Prison. He had found out I had rode in and was so happy to see me. He also knew that I was a problem and it would be just a matter of time before I had set this facility off as I did every other location. He would be on my head like "all that stuff I been hearing about you doing that's dead!" He had been at Earth for a little while. He had be respected by all as usual, so the officers had backed off me. I still wasn't able to be around him all the way. He would beg me to move on his side of the unit I'm like bro I'm on something. I didn't want to be around him just yet because I had some unfinished business. I had gotten a jpay from this female that claimed her baby daddy had gave her my information. So I had reached back out. It was the guy who had wanted me to ghostwrite for his baby mama. She had got with me which showed me that she was serious about working with me. I had got a phone number and we would just build and talk about the industry. She had a buzz in her little city which made it easier to establish a footing in the game. She had already been working with producers like Honorable C-Note. I had been aware of Honorable C-Notes work because he worked with a lot of platinum artist like Young Dolph, Migos etc. I was ambitious and excited about this opportunity to be back doing what I loved most. Music! I had been building with my lil brother RocstarTwun. We would make plans on establishing a record label and making it to an industry level. He had been close friends with 42 Dugg who is signed with YoGotti/CMG. Lil Dugg even had been working with the artist Lil Baby that had hit the industry strong. So I saw it as a huge opportunity to get in position. I had also been connected with my big homie who had ties to Helluva. What made this such a difficult thing for me was I loved this producers work. But I ?knew that I'd never be forgiven for my actions. Even being completely unaware of who people I had harmed. I had only hoped that guys see that I had accepted my consequences and had been put in prison behind the event. Extend Grace. I remember being nearly in tears when I had sat alone in my cell while my bunk mate had been on yard. I didn't understand what God had in store for me. I had left my dream to come to prison and oddly I was somehow connected to my victims brother mutually. I was optimistic though. I just wanted to do music. I didn't have any ill intentions or animosity toward Helluva. And from the few sources I had been associated with, he hadn't had non towards me. Thus, I jumped on the opportunity to showcase my talents. I had grown close to the female artist I was working with. Harbor Quinn was a phenomenal artist. I saw so much potential in her. I would began writing all kinds of music for her. I wrote almost fortysomething songs. In the midst of us doing business it somehow crossed the line into uncharted territory. I had plugged her with my big homie who had stepped into the picture. I had only been the ghostwriter plus I didn't have the direct plugs he had to some heavy hitter in the music industry.

    Harbor Quinn, and I had started building a bond outside of the business. I hadn't anticipated such affection that I would develop for her but it heated up pretty fast. She had kept cutting into me about things that was not related to the music. I was trying to keep it professional as possible. I would seek advice from my guy Rocstar. He was against it because he had thought it would mess the business up and we had planned on pushing her as our first female artist. Rocstar was approaching his outdate and we had become very close. His family had grew up with my father's siblings. I even grew up on Rohns with some of his cousins. I had embraced him as family. So I valued his opinion, but I did not heed his advice. Even my big homie was against it. I saw how much I had been consumed with the woman life. I had invested so much time and creativity into her that I didn't want to lose her. We both fell head over hills. I had thought about what her baby daddy would say about our relationship, however, I didn't own him any loyalty. She had told me all the things he put her through and she had made her decision to establish an intimate bond. We had got so deep in this love thing that I had been like a fish out of water. Most of my bid I went without pursuing women. After me and Ashley had fell out, I figured it would be a weakness so I ridded myself of the desire to beloved or share my affection with some woman who in turn would hurt me because I couldn't be there physically. So I only allowed myself to love only one things and that was this thing of ours. The lifestyle was my distraction. It was my family and it shielded me from the pain of being let down by my family, friends and significant others. I refused to be the guy on the phone questioning where his woman was at last night, or who she had been laying? I had only prepared myself for that special woman. I read all sorts of books on relationship. One of my favorite books is Real Love by Sister Ava Muhammad. I would use her book as a manual to cultivate our relationship. I had become Harbor Quinn crutch. She basically did her bid off me. The whole time the pandemic was active and people couldn't do what they wanted to do we were engaged all kind of stuff. I thought our love was real. But some women just going to act outside their nature. I had finally gotten a chance to move on the same rock as my big homie. We had immediately got to work. He would have me writing music all day. We would build on building something everlasting. I had still been active with the lifestyle. He understood that because he knew the troubles that came with being on that. He was about getting money, staying out the way and off the radar. I remember one day we had a talk about me being on nonsense. He had told me that I had a multimillionaire mind with a broke niggas mentality. I was hurt. We had stopped talking for like two days. But he was right. My focus was in the wrong place. He would see me caking with Harbor Quinn all day instead of being in the war room with him trying to figure out how we could get rich and get our freedom back. I remember one day we were sitting at chow. The subject had come up about Helluva. I could see he was conflicted and torn between the two. I even hated the fact that this was a part of my story. I remember he had told me something that I never will forget and I'd always live by, "I would never do for money, that I won't do for free." That was such a powerful declaration. That meant so much to me and what was understood didn't need to be explained. His love was real for me and from that day I'm not even sure if he knows this, I said I will do everything in my power to get in position so I can help get him out of prison. The streets need a big homie like him. He was way more valuable to the communities and if I had guys like him guiding me along with my other village, I'd possibly been in a better position. After predicting that Harbor Quinn was going to play me, my big homie started encouraging me to start back rapping. He like, "nigga you keep talking about writing an doing things for all these other people when you really the truth. You the one!" I looked him in his eyes and seen that he meant every word he said and that was all I needed to see was someone that I love/respect to believe in my God given talent's. He had staged a challenge in tribute to Helluva and 42 Dugg Habits beat that was on the Young & Turnt 2(Deluxe) album. I had written some bars and my big homie was in awe. He had instantly made it official that I was doing music if he had anything to do with it. I had slayed Helluva beat. I had even shouted him out despite the conflict of interest. Of course with all good things guys see you doing things they can't do, jealously kicks in. The Honorable Minister Louis Farrakhan teaches us that Jealousy destroys within. Boy was he not lying. I had got into a fight with one of my so-called homies walking to chow. I remember my big homie like "come on nigga forget them niggas." Guys had been mad that I would be on the phone the whole yard when they didn't have the funds to do so.

But this was also what my big homie anticipated that's why he would be on me about being out the caking, stuck up girls behind. Harbor Quinn had been on her way to Atlanta to work with Honorable C-Note and shoot a video to one of songs I wrote for her. We had made sure we booked her some performances etc. There I was making power moves like that but fighting with guys over something I could've avoided. Even if I had just fell back on the lifestyle and focused on me I would've not had these setbacks.

    I had gotten released from segregation and was housed on an entire different wing. My big homie was so mad because I had messed up that time we had to build up and just strengthen our bond. I was so disappointed but I refused to allow someone to disrespect me. Less than a week I had gotten some devastating news. I had lost three important people in my life. All to natural causes. One of those beloved family members was my cousin Kim. My cousin Kim had passed away and the family was struggling trying together enough money to lay her in peace. Kim had been one of my favorite people. She had always looked out for me as a kid. Thus I wanted her to be put to rest properly. I hated hearing that her body was at the morgue while we had family that could've easily paid for her funereal. Me being me I couldn't let her go without. I had contacted my mother and asked how much money they needed to cover the bill. I had had a few dollars that I was saving up and planning to invest in an attorney to get out of here, here it was I had to take money from that to do something my family could've done. At this time Harbor Quinn had ghosted me. She had got all the things she needed to excel and the shelter in place had been lifted after quarantine. She had all my money that I hustled up on and jugged up. We had been saving together. She had been in Atlanta spending my money we shared and accumulated together on Pink face Rolex watches and diamond custom made chains. I understood that that was a part of her career. She couldn't just get in the game simply off her bars. She had way to much competition. I had even been propositioned to write a song for Cartie B after my big homie had lined up a potential ghostwriting deal. I'm not sure why I didn't take that serious. It had to be because I had been gone over Harbor Quinn and wanted to push her career. I felt like if I had written a hit for her and it blew up, that could've been my artist. I still had that business perspective along with the suck a mentality I had forher. Of course I still was doing what I do with my lifestyle. I had did exactly what I did at every other spot. Most guys made me out to be this Warmonger. That honestly wasn't the case, I just stood on my beliefs and made sure everybody else did as well. One guy that I had held accountable for his transgressions rocked me to sleep. I had been so used to being the aggressor or the person that strike first that I had been caught lacking. I remember walking up the stairs writing a jpay to Harbor Quinn seeking answers as to why she just upped and ghosted me. I had got to the top of the stairs and all I remember was feeling like I had been in a car accident. The individual that I had held accountable, had made a pact with me. He told me he had a parole and I wasn't the kind of guy to keep someone in prison. So I gave him a pass, however, he had been laying on me. He had punched me so hard in the mouth that my tooth had splintered thru my top lip. I hadn't never bleed so much in my life. In fact it had been like fifteen years since I had lost a fight yet alone been hit. I was so good with boxing that guys rarely hit me. Boy did he wake me up. I didn't drop or fall but I had lunged toward him to fight and out of nowhere the Correctional officers tased and gassed me. When the volts had hit my body I hit the ground face first. My tooth had been knocked out and I laid in a pool of my own blood. I could feel the blood squirting from my lip as the taser had sent electrical currents through my body causing every muscle in my body to tense. I just remember looking down at my clothes. My whole white t-shirt and brand new white Nike's had been drenched in blood. My tooth was left behind and parts of it was in my lip still. I could only do nothing but thank God. I promise you I was so Thankful for that experience because I just thought, MAN THATCOULD'VE BEEN MY LIFE. IF THIS WAS THE WORLDAND I HAD BEEN AMBUSHED LIKE THAT ITWOULD'VE BEEN OVER BEFORE I EVEN REALIZED. What a Wakeup call...?

Chapter 18 IN DIS CELL (MOST OF MY LIFE)

"As You Seek Your Way In The World, Never Fail To Find A Way To Serve Your Community. Use Your Education And Your Success In Life To Help Those Still Trapped In Cycles Of Poverty And Violence ."-Colin L. Powell I had Arrived back at Marquette Branch Prison January 2021. After the situation with the guy that had snuck me at Earth, I had been placed on involuntary protection and transferred to Maximum Security. I was so confused. I had never needed any protection from the administration, however, due to my rap sheet and the administration being oblivious as to why I had been assaulted, they thought keeping me in segregation was for my wellbeing. I had that don't help me help the Grizzly Bear mentality. But what was really funny about the transfer was the fact that I was the victim for once in my life and I still had been classified to maximum security. Come to find out, I was supposed to had been sent to a level four facility, but the receiving facility refused to accept me on their compound because my reputation. I had been housed in Bravo block. I didn't trip about being back in max. It was almost as if I had been on a leash. It had been three years since I had last been back in the higher security level. After going through the covid protocols, I had been able to be placed on general population. Covid-19 had not yet reached Marquette Branch like it did every other facility. I had been up on the second gallery reunited withal my homies. Guys had relayed to me all the things I had been doing down state. Some stories were over exaggerated, some never occurred but one thing for sure I had made a lot of noise. Being that most of my guys were stuck in maximum security prisons, I had to be able to stand on my own which allowed me to create a household name. Everybody heard aboutSuperbadd37.I had immediately began to mobilize and educate my brothers on all the new things I've learned. I had so many resources and made some great connections with some huge assets. Before I had left my big homie had linked me with one of his guys that had been released after serving 23 years in the MDOC. He had been helping me record music for the first time since I was free in prison. I had written this song titled NIGGAS DATS NOT. It had sounded so good. I had also turned the bars I had written for the Habit challenge that we did with my big homie in tribute to Helluva and 42 Dugg, in to an actual song titled BADHABITS.I had been back in touch with my guys in the world and I was just bringing a new edition to my brothers. We had been doing so much all over the state and we needed some positive results. I had to change the trajectory of what we were doing. It was met with opposition as usual. I understood exactly why though. Despite being Superb add I still had guys whispering about my past. I didn't let it stop me though. Nothing would get in my way. My cousin Kim's son had started reaching out to me. He had been doing music. Come to find out he had quite the buzz in the city

IN DIS CELL DEANGELO ANTHONY

of Memphis, Tennessee with over a million view's collectively on YouTube. He was famous in his own right and he had been working with the platinum producer Zaytoven and he had been rumored working on signing with Future. Thus, it was like the music dream was coming tenfold. I had moved on somewhat over Harbor Quinn. I would still promote her work because I had wanted to see her shine. Plus she had been in contact with one of my homies, he'd keep me posted on her progress. There had been a huge riot at Chippewa Correctional Facility. The correction officers had shot an inmate in the face with a taser and it went up into an uproar. My big homie had been in Nemours unit around the time. So he had got wrapped up in that and we had lost contact. The administration had a mass ride in with all the guys I just left at the previous facility. The whole Earth had rode into Marquette Branch Prison it seemed like. Let me tell you how they played these guys. First all their personal property had been destroyed. Secondly they had been housed in a block that hadn't been habitable since like 2012. It had black mold everywhere. So they housed these prisoners in Charlie block during a pandemic. We all know that black mold alone is a hazardous environment but add one of the deadliest viruses known to humanity in the mix. Those guys had been gassed and treated so inhumane you'd think they had rioted at Marquette Branch Prison the way they retaliated towards them. Around October 4th, 2021 I had contracted the virus. I just remember feeling so weak and all five of my senses were abnormal. I had told the nurses about my symptoms and during this time the virus had not yet reached Marquette Branch Prison. I was told that I had no worries it was only a flu it would pass. My head had been hurting. I couldn't hear it felt like I was in an airplane or something. I didn't have an appetite. When I would prepare for sleep I would literally pled to God to allow me to wake up the following day. I remember waking up in shivers and cold sweats. I was under every clothing item and bed spread I had and was still freezing. I remember telling myself like DEANGELO YOU ABOUT TO DIE... DAMN, THIS IS IT. Like I really felt like that.

Due to all year around air circulation systems spreading germs, other guys had been feeling the same exact systems. One guy had an underlined health disorder. He had a c-pap machine. The fan blew whatever bacteria's we sneezed or coughed into the air. The administration had failed to protect us from the virus by allowing some irresponsible correction officer to work knowing they were sick and displaying symptoms. I must admit though, they barely had staffing because people were dropping like flies. The death toll was so high and the number of people that had contracted the virus had been placed on quarantine status. The MDOC had established a new Covid-19Protocol that mandated that all prisoners that had been positive for Covid-19 had to be emergency transferred to St. Louis Correctional Facilities Covid Unit. The National Guard had been deployed to Marquette Branch Prison and other facilities in the state of Michigan and did a mass Covid-19 testing campaign. We had been told either we take the test or be placed in segregation for fourteen days. It didn't matter whether we refused the test or not, the entire compound had been placed on lock down because there was a huge outbreak. Giving the benefit of the doubt, it was an experience not even the worlds renowned Scientists were ready for. Every country had been shut down it looked like the end of the world. Dooms Day! I remember telling myself like THISCOULDN'T HAVE BEEN SOME MADMAN IN CHINATHAT ATE A BAT AND THE WHOLE WORLD ENDEDUP SICK. HELL NAW, THIS SOMEEXTRATERRESTRIAL TYPE STUFF. It was something straight out of the biblical text. I had been of the first wave of prisoners that had been positive for Covid-19. I was packed up and told I would be riding out to the Covid-19 unit in St. Louis to protect the other prisoners. However, they placed me in Charlie block with the prisoners from Chippewa. Most of those guys were negative for Covid-19. What sense did it make to place me and several other level5 prisoners around negative prisoners other than to get them sick as well? Right! By the time we knew it the entire location had become an epicenter for the virus. 900 plus prisoners including staff had been positive for the virus. The administration had taken a horde immunity approach that had been only observed by the Republican Ron Paul. It was a terrible philosophy. After doing may be a couple weeks on quarantine status, I had been placed on step down and moved to Golf block which was also on quarantine status.

I remember asking the former warden Erika Huss why hadn't I been transferred? Her reply was she needed everyone to contract the virus so we'd have immunity. That was absurd. Less than a week on my step down status I had collapsed at my cell door unconscious. One of the porters had been stopped by my neighbor and they were throwing water on me all kind of things trying to get an reaction. It had been said that I wasn't breathing and the medical staff had been called. They said that the nurse refused to perform CPR because she couldn't do mouth to mouth. Now here it was I didn't have a pulse nor was I responding to any of the things they did to get a reaction. Look as much of a Guerilla (George Jackson) I am, this was the first time I can say I was thankful for the Correctional officers that had come to my aid. Two male officers had sprung into action and did CPR. They had used four doses of Narcan everything possible and luckily they had arrived because they saved my life. I had been rushed to the hospital offsite in the EMS. After a series of test using EKG and having all kind of tubes taped to both arms, I woke up back in prison as if it were a bad dream!...Okay, I'm not a medical physician but if you don't have a pulse nor heartbeat, doesn't that mean your scientifically dead? How on God's green earth did I wake up in the same exact prison cell I had been found unresponsive in? I didn't even have a medical follow up until my neighbor cut into the nurse on my behalf. They had did two EKG's and determined that from the effects of the Covid-19 virus it had caused fluid to be on my heart and I suffered from quote-on-quote, 'respiratory suppression.' Whatever the hell that is? After seeing that my life had been at risk, I knew that I had to take life way more serious. I refused to die in prison and after such close call and seeing how they didn't even care about me, I sprang into action. I had to do it for Lil Mook, the others and myself that died in the care of the MDOC. I called my mother and told her about it. I asked her to record my phone call and forward it to a reporter named Angela Jacksonwith The Detroit Free Press. That following week an article had been published exposing the negligence and reckless disregard of prisoners lives at Marquette Branch Prison. The epicenter...I can't lie, that article along with a host of other things made it hard for the Correctional officers. They had been catching all hell. Every other day they had been assaulted by inmates for whatever reasons. One of those events I had ended up being caught up in. A couple of my brothers had took justice into their own hands after one of the guys had been gassed. The brother had one lung and several underlined health disorders. Anyhow, I had caught a failure to disburse along with multiple other prisoners that had taken the yard hostage because of how the administration responded and stood on one of my brothers neck right after the Eric Garner murder in Minnesota. So tension was high. Guards were even firing live rounds at us. Yeah it was a mess.

In segregation I had begun to read George Jacksons Soledad Brothers and Bishop T.D. Jakes (The Crushing if I'm not mistaken). It had been my second time reading this powerful revolutionary book. I knew that we could not win by assaulting the officers. That had been done and nothing but unwanted attention came from it. Thus, I wanted to use my mind to defeat them. The power of the pen. I had received more bad news. My beloved grandmother Pastor Arizona Jenkins had been on her death bed. I had been allowed to use the phone. I remember talking to her and hearing how she was so joyful and optimistic about going on to the lord Jesus Christ. It wasn't a hint of fear or worry in her. While she was laughing and being her normal self, I was in a single man cell crying like a baby. I was able to speak with her right before she had passed away...After my grandmother passed it really did something to me. That on top of all that I had experienced was just like, damn. I have to get home. I've missed so much and I just had to get this time off of me. My mother had hired me an attorney and they started trying to push a Motion For Compassion. However, that was denied due to me being in the state prison system. Only the federal inmates were lucky enough to get out on that motion. Being forced inside The Start Program which is for long term segregation, however, the administration found a way to exploit it by placing major mental disorderly prisoners in the program. I had not wanted to go because a lot of prisoners sort of hideout there. I couldn't have that on my name but my brothers felt I needed that time off. I had been there trying to get my mind right. My grandmother's funeral had been held the day of me entering the program. I had been able to attend over the phone. I could hear my cousin Joi reading the letter that I had written for my grandmother and family. My daughter had been blessed with an opportunity I had never been able to experience. She was able to meet and actually have a relationship with her great grandmother. That was cool to me because I was talking to my daughter during the service. She was relating everything to me. My daughter is so much like me. She like my little twin. She bad as heck. It's funny how life works. She had been nicknamed 'Bad Butt' and I had earned the moniker Superb add. I swear I hadn't known this until her mother told me that her other child's father that had been raising my daughter while I been incarcerated named her that because she was so bad. My daughter very sneaky but highly intelligent. I love talking to because she always played everybody else for a fool but she knew that she could get things over me. I knew she was smart and knew how to manipulate her way through life because I'm sure she inherited that trait from me. Believe it or not my daughter taught me how to respect ad accept the new world. I had been brought up in the system where we did look down on homosexuality. I had found out how hypersexual the world had become when I held a conversation with my daughter about her sexual preference. I remember my daughter asking me a question indirectly. She said, "daddy... can I ask you a question? "I had replied, "of course Myonna. You know we can talk about anything."

Boy did she drop a bomb on me. She continued to say after a short pause as she strategically chose her words, "I know this girl. She my friend and she like girls. She finds them attractive. What you think about that daddy?" Me being very conscious of what I say to her, I knew that I couldn't lie to make her feel better. I had told her that I personally don't agree with same sex relationships but I would not judge that person nor disown them or treat them less than who they are. I waited for her response. This is how I knew she was very intelligent and had matured into this beautiful teenager. The ways he pondered and reflected and analyzed everything. The Minister Louis Farrakhan said one must think five times before they speak so that they doesn't say anything ignorant and what they does not mean. I knew she was trying to find a way to tell me that friend was her. So I had helped her with it. I said, "you know once upon a time your aunty Me on had been like that when she was your age but that was a phase-" She had interjected, "what if it ain't a phase?"That's when I knew she was serious about her preference because only someone who has made their mind up would rebuttal with such response. I remember sitting in my bed listening to Rod Wave "Pray For Love" saying, MAN MY DAUGHTER IS GAY. I had then told myself that I had to accept this new day and age without being bias. Whatever someone wanted to do with their life and they following their true self whether it goes against the laws of nature, you have to accept them for exactly who they show you they are. Otherwise passing judgment would be a form of hypocrisy especially if you still committing sins yourself. Sin is Sin. To me be mine, to you be yours.

When I finally gained control over my emotions, I had signed off the program to go back to General Population. When I got out I was placed in Golf block. I had finished reading the Soledad Brothers and upgraded my mind state to combat fascism. I had linked with one of my guys who had been the pioneer for Michigan with recording over the phone. Boss Hogg Bud had plugged everybody with a producer named Goat Town E. He had been charging us a little of nothing to record quality music over the prison phone and upload the music to the kiosk. I had paid him $150 dollars to record two songs. Me and one of the guys No good Daybook had collaborated on the song I had written originally for the Helluva challenge Bad Habits and I dropped Niggas That's Not. It felt so good to be able to go upload my own songs that had sounded so good to my JP6 tablet. It was a new niche market and we were creating away to be able to finally do something positive to get our names up instead of being active on these yards. I remember looking up and my song Bad Habits had been all over the state on guys tablets. I was getting some great responses for the song even people in the world loved my music. That was all I needed and the rest would be history.

CHAPTER 19 IN DIS CELL (MOST OF MY LIFE)

"By Profession I Am A Solider And Take Pride In That Fact. But I Am Prouder - Infinitely Prouder - To Be A Father. A Solider Destroys In Order To Build; The Father Only Builds, Never Destroy. The One Has The Potentiality Of Death; The Other Embodies Creation And Life. And While The Hordes Of Death Are Mighty, The Battalions Of Life Are Mightier Still. It Is My Hope That My Son, When I Am Gone, Will Remember Me Not From The Battle Field But In The Home Repeating With Him Our Simple Daily Prayer, 'Our Father Who Art In Heaven'. "-Douglas MacArthur When the year 2022 had rolled in I had been on a rampage. After absorbing so much revolutionary reading material, I had radicalized myself. I had been doing so much in my community. The first thing I did was go with every respected group and pulled them together due to the fact we had been fighting each other but the real oppressors was the system. So we all banded together and proceeded to establish a pact that had been so powerful that we managed to draw lines on the prison yard. At one point there was so many staff assaults. Every other day a guard had been injured physically. I had believed that using the pen was the power but I had later found that there had never been a revolution fought without the shedding of blood. Our blood had been shed every day nearly. We didn't hesitate to bring harm to one another. Whether I had agreed with the physical aspect of the revolution, I knew that if we had properly communicated what we wanted to happen to the administration, only then we would get some positive results from our negative actions. After being the prisoner to defuse several events where things could've gotten out of hand with staff and prisoners, I had been identified as the one who was more diplomatic amongst my peers. Thus, every time things seemed to arise the officers would come to me and give us a chance to govern ourselves. I had been organizing brothers from all walks of life and we would go to them and we would talk it out and in turn there would be a solution that was nonviolent. The system I had organized worked. I didn't want to keep seeing people get hurt and I darn sure didn't want to keep seeing prisoners jack rec over something that could have been resolved. Now of course all situations didn't end so peaceful but most of them did. I had the food clerk of Golf block. And another individual that was a student of Larry Hoover had been the Housing Unit Clerk. We had started hiring brothers and making sure our living quarters was clean. When guys had been hired whether it been as a porter or kitchen worker, we would set rules and make sure they knew that it was for the betterment of the environment. With such discipline the administration had been willing to turn a blind eye. We kept our politics behind closed doors and out the eyes of the public. However, one of the higher administrative staff had visited our block and seen how peaceful things were and wanted to know how the block became so chill. There wasn't any fights, stabbings nor staff assaults without sanctions. But the administration actually relied on the prisoner on prisoner violence because it kept the prisoners busy with one another while the administration sat back and watched us destroy one another. I had remember seeing them make a move by switching up the staffing for over familiarization. They had placed some real douch bags into the block. There was this one young officer newly hired in and he wanted to make his bones. He would be so disrespectful and figured if he poked his chest out it would help him look stronger than the others. The environment wasn't even on being at odds with the officers in our block. However, I had got into a verbal altercation with him and it had went as dar as him trying to square up with me. Now I'm thinking this guy must be crazy and have a death wish because he in an environment where guys didn't care less what happened especially, after witnessing millions die from covid.

  Realizing the mentality of this individual I had understood that I couldn't feed into his hand. Even his fellow coworkers disagreed with his unprofessional behavior. He had been escorted out of the unit and the officers were so scared because they knew the caliber individuals they were dealing with. Plus I am a very respectful individual. I'm yes sir; No Sir; Good Morning and a Thank You kind of guy. I didn't have an authority issue unless the authority was abused. I understand I am in prison and in prison the guards are law. But I only followed Gods law which states all human beings are equal. Honor thy neighbor. Do onto people as you'd do onto yourself. This is when the administration saw that may be I had too much influence. After the officer had been taken out for a cool down the rum who is the housing manager had called a sit down with me and two other prisoners along with the shift commander. We had an open dialogue where I was allowed to speak freely as well as the officer. Of course I knew that it was imperative that I articulated myself professionally. After stating my stance, I had respectfully allowed the officer to speak and analyzed his perspectives. The guy was so far right and indoctrinated with fascist beliefs I then knew that I was dealing with something bigger than us. He had been a mole for the administration to dismantle the environment and create that tension to gain back full control. After exposing that kind of influence and power, I had officially became a target. The administration would go to play Cointellpro (Counter Intelligence Program) games as if we were ignorant of their tactics. Well, I and possibly a few others didn't fall for the divide and conquer game but they had created such a riff amongst my house that brothers started to turn on me. Divided we fall. After getting into another run in with this one officer the administration had moved me from Golf block to Bravo block where there was so many chiefs and not enough Indians. It was so disorient in this block. Don't get me wrong there was structure but nobody had been on the same page. I had been dethroned and from there I fell back. One of our drop outs had begun to build a smear campaign on my name. It had ultimately ended with me taking a trip to segregation. When I had got out of segregation I had a medical issue. I had a hernia in my abdominal area. I had to get it surgically patched up which had me down and disabled. The officers had saw me deteriorating both physically and influentially. They saw it as a chance to mess me over. I had not been able to walk and I was placed on the gallery. Walking to showers was the most painful experience I ever had. Plus, it was so chaotic that it was a safety hazard for me to be moving freely around other inmates. I would see the officers and other inmates watching me like vultures. Yeah, I looked like prey once again. However, there was some guys that still had love for me. Actually there was a lot of guys that had love for me and they had made a huge sense because I kept having blood in my stool. I didn't know what was going on. I had been on some percosets for pain. I didn't know that pain pills could cause you to have blood in your stool. I had been moved to a base cell. One of the guys had personally cleaned my cell for me after having to argue with the officers because they expected me to be able to clean my own cell in excruciating pain. I couldn't even move nor bend over. I remember laying there up in the middle of the night just thinking. I had been back around Boss Hogg Bud and another guy we met from the Feds Sony P whose brother had produced for A Boogie Wit DaHoodie. We had linked up on the music tip. My little cousin Migo Money had died shortly after his mother Kim, and his death moved me to take the music to another level. I had started writing four to five songs a day. Boss Hogg would come to my cell and hear me rapping and he had offered me a seat at their table. They had been establishing 4eva Epic Entertainment. We had obtained an Empire Distribution deal and from the prison yard we had been recording music dropping it on the kiosk. So I'm sitting up late at night. At Marquette Branch Prison they shut the power off at twelve o'clock sharp. On the 'you ever had to go night night nigga?' (Kevin Hart voice).I had begun to get in my feelings. I was high as hell off the pain pills I was taking. I'm laying on my back and it's like my whole life flashed before me. I had walked through my childhood and when I had reached the point in life where I thought about my son I began to cry. My children had become victims of my actions because I abandoned them. I thought about what my son would think of me? I had lost respect for my father and became angry with him for abandoning me before I had entered the world. He wasn't there to see me come out of my mother's womb. He wasn't there to hear my first words. Witness my first steps. See me off to school or take me to the park to play catch or teach me some sport. He had left me in the womb. But what made me start to forgive my father and wanted to mend our relationship was when I thought about my son Deandre. He had been subjected to the same exact thing. Everything that I would be able to say about my father he could say the same about me.

    This vicious cycle that had seemed to be every young black males story, had now reached my son. Genocide at its finest. We often are told that it's not about race or gentrification, when if you look at our communities you'd see that the black man is only promised two things; Death or jail! 'All the real niggas either dead or in jail/if you looking for me niggas I'm in the ATL/' (Young Jeezy).Society has placed this cloud over us which strikes every generation we produce. We have to come to prison almost just to obtain the knowledge of self. It took me to experience prison simply to save my life when my community is that bad to the point our parents believe this to be true. How is it so, that people would feel comfortable telling their loved ones that prison saved their life? What

IN DIS CELL DEANGELO ANTHONY

about God? What about Education? What about Opportunity? What about equal rights? I do not want this for my son. I had walked literally down the same wide path of my father. I been on the same prison yards and possibly the same prison cells as he. I would talk to my father about his experience in prison and it would be as if he was relating exactly what I am dealing with. Verbatim! So I had this smooth beat playing that Payday J had produced 'Get Together' and I began to write; Locked off in Dis cell got me crushing down these blues/ feeling all this pain, barely can take of my shoes/ working on my heart, you can tell that it been bruised/ I done gave my love and loyalty and been misused/ if you fool me once den nigga dats shame on you/ and if it happens twice den may be your someone's fool/ gotta learn your lesson like you were still in school/ steel sharpen steel betta stay around dem tools/(Chorus)Dis for my son I want my lil nigga game tight/ cause when he grow up I know he gon have da same fight/ I know I ain't been around nearly yo' whole life/ an yeah I been on dat yard bangin dat ol' knife/ I'm such a lowlife/ yo' uncle Jeremi praying dat I get my soul right/dey working on my appeal I hope it goes right/ but if it ain't in God's plan, its gon be alright/ Just know your daddy a dog and its a dog fight/ it ain't da size of dadog, gotta big fight in me/ and I been through what you been through come confine in me/ an I gottashine bright, but in time you'll see/(verse)Locked off in Dis cell got me crushing down these blues/ feeling all this pain, barely can take of my shoes/ working on my heart, you can tell that it been bruised/ I done gave my love and loyalty and been misused/ if you fool me once den nigga dats shame on you/ and

IN DIS CELL DEANGELO ANTHONY

if it happens twice den may be your someone's fool/ gotta learn your lesson like you were still in school/ steel sharpen steel betta stay arounddem tools/(chorus)I had remembered thinking man I'm In Dis Cell writing this song for my son, whether I record it inhere or twenty years from now imma make sure he hears it. Thus, I named it "In Dis Cell." I also had written several other songs in the course of me being on bed rest. My mental health handler Mrs. Bailey-Webb had always been in my corner. When I would breakdown mentally she would be there to lift me up. She had reminded me of my grandmother. This white lady had so much love, care and concern for me professionally that I felt comfortable with expressing how I feel wither. I had no issue telling her about my life. Sometimes when I would relay my story to her as we sought to address my past trauma, I would even cry and she'd tell me to get it out its healthy. She was my angel. I had a safe haven with her. She had been my counselor for years since I've been at Marquette Branch. I had never trusted in someone so much, especially with my pain as I did with her. Mrs. Bailey-Webb had been there for me every step of the way and she would always make sure I had the best of treatment. I didn't even think mental health was real. Nor did I respect qualified mental healthcare staff because I thought it was all about textbook and medication. However, I worked through some real life issues simply by just communicating without fear. I recommend anyone that is suffering from mental health to deeply consider seeking help and really taking advantage of those people who studied years to be able to help people like us. After a few setbacks the mental health treatment decided that I needed a more hands on treatment without all the nonsense that took the attention off of me being able to focus on my problems. I had been referred to the Residential Treatment program once again.

Chapter 20 IN DIS CELL (MOST OF MY LIFE)

"A Wise Man Said 'A Bad Plan Is Better Than No Plan.'"-Kent Marvel's Black Adam I remember being on the bus heading to RTP around April 2022. My lil homie had been on his way downstate to participate in the program as well. I hadn't been around the lil homie since we were last at Carson City 2019. He had been mobbing back then before he had stepped outside his mandates. However, despite his sins I had still had brotherly love for the young guy because he had always been willing to stand on his actions. He had more honor than most guys when they had violated the rules. Most guys would run from the consequences but Boosie ran to them. When I had heard about his extra curriculum activities I had been so disappointed. I never known him to be going that way but what I thought I knew had changed. He kept it real though and let me know. After telling me what he had been up to, the homie asked me whatever penalty I decided to issue he would take it like a man. You don't hear guys talk like that. He actions were punishable by death according to the streets but we were in prison and guys wasn't trying to lock themselves in. Nevertheless, there was other ways more convenient and suitable for his willingness to accept his fate. Also I had been communicating with his mother and she had been one of the biggest kingpins(T-Stucky) baby mama out the city. Plus, I had been building with his daughter and we had this soul mate type vibe. She was everything I ever wanted in a woman. The caliber female that I needed had to be a thoroughbred. She was so beautiful and intelligent tome. I just fell in love with her on sight. So with those ties and rapports I had been cultivating I didn't want to see him be physically harmed even though he was subjected to it. We signed up for something and when you step outside of those boundaries you must be held accountable. He had been fortunate enough to come up on some major pape. He had always known me to be doing music. I had been sharing my plans with him and he had offered to fund my career as a silent investor. Originally I was hesitant because I knew how to make my own way. I had all the resources to be successful but to be able to bypass the extra logistics and hurdles I made the best business decision possible. After asking me to reiterate my plan, he listened very carefully and said, "Alo I believe in you. I got ten know that I had the financial backing I needed to neutralize the environment. I had enough influence that I would be able to get the brothers to let him alone on my behalf. We had arrived at Macomb Correctional Facility. Well he had made it their first then I came a couple weeks later as I anticipated. I had went to Gus Harrison once again but the fact that I had been fighting a law suit over the situation I experienced, they found it as a conflict of interest for me to be there. I remember riding into Macomb Correctional Facility. It felt so good to be so close to the city. I had never been so lucky. Last time I didn't last sixty days at Macomb before I had been on an emergency ride out because the homies popped off. Now I was back there with a better mind state. I had a plan and I would stop at nothing to execute as planned. I was told, 'aman without a plan, plans to fail. 'When I had arrived everything had been Taylor made. How we got the cellphones was neither here nor there. But what we decided to do with the phones was what mattered. I had been locking in cell 33 with my brother Treezy. Homie and I would build all day every day on the music industry. We both had strong ties to people who had been connected in the world. I had reached out to my resources and since we had the device to record our own vocals, mix and master them all I needed was someone to add the finishing touches. I only knew one man that would be able to help me with what I aimed to accomplish. I got ahold to my uncle T-Grymee and he linked me with my old producer that produced my first real studio EP when I was signed with Grymee Records. Melodic Beats was a master at what he did. I would forward the vocals to him and he'd build beats around the vocals. I also was able to reach out to some of my guys that was doing music. My brother Rocstar Tw unlinked me with one of his guys that had been running their label Dog food Records/Family Fed Entertainment. My guy CEO Spazz had vibed with me and Treezy off bell. He had just been in the same predicament we had been in so he knew what we needed. CEO Spazz had this hot producer out the city Paid Chill. We had did a song called Good fellas (Pauly) and we sent the song to Paid Chill. Man when we heard the new version of the song it was mind blowing. He had made this funky NWA type sound, that had the hard bass kicking. The piano was all over the place I mean this guy was a musical genius! CEO Spazz had added his musical genius to the song by adding a skit from the movie Good fellas and from their I knew we had the perfect team to acquire success.

Anyhow, we would literally make like twenty songs a day free styling to the point Rap Fame had changed their algorithm where they added a limit to how many songs you could publish. We still found ways around their guidelines. We was going viral all over the place. The Rapper Jada Kiss was even popping at us through Rap Fame trying to get us to enter this co test he was hosting. We had all sorts of people trying to link with us and do features. We was blazing the trail and people began to take notice of our work ethic. Also we had been building with one of the homie girls Nefertiti. We'd call her and tag her in on our Instagram Live. She would post all our music and store songs for us. Nefertiti aka Brooke hands down is the realest female I know. She solid. She had did a bid at Huron Valley and when she got out she had been all for helping people who had been in her struggle. Our first time talking to Brooke we was on face time with her. She had been in the passenger seat of a Meseriti with her wire frames on. She had been with the rapper Boldy James that is signed with ROC Nation and another well-known producer. The boys had been dripping with big chucky diamond BMF chains. She like, "look these my brothers in prison they in there tripping!" We had rapped for them and they was likely' all boys hot. "The last piece to the puzzle was JT Beatz. I had connected with him through one of the students of Tookie, my man's 31third. We had did a song with him and I found that he also did videos. So I had finally been able to share the final aspect to our plan. We had told him we was going to shoot a real music video and if so could he help structure it for us. He like yeah just send me the clips and I'll get with my guy and we'd see what y'all come up with. That's all we needed to hear. Before we decided to actually record the video we had first made sure we completed our album. I remember we told Melodic like yeah we wanna do aEP. He like "bro do seven songs because you could be nominate for a Grammy." We was like this nigga said we can get a Grammy! He had that much faith in our talent. We was putting the work in and people started to see the fruits of our labors. Hard work pays off. I remember we had cleaned up our cell. We had went had one of the guys on the yard line us up. I made sure we had crispy blues. We stayed prison fresh we had so many pairs of shoes it was ridiculous. It was like we had the whole catalog so we had enough to really clean up well. It's like all the things I thought about doing started to happen. We got the red bandana so we can show the love for the lifestyle. It was amazing. I had been did videos when I was free so I knew exactly what we had to do. Treezy had never did a music video ever. It took my brother to come to prison to do one. However, my man's was photogenic! He had mapped out his own clips. He like "Imma do this or that". I'm like "imma go up here, sit right there". We literally directed our own music video in one prison cell. The first version of the video JT Beatz had put it together but he like, " I think y'all need to add some more clips. Do something different. I know y'all in one cell but figure something else out may be put some pictures etc." I had pondered so hard me and Treezy like what else can we do? You would've thought we conjured this next part into existence because it had happened to be what made the video so powerful. The unit had been placed on lockdown after an inmate had went to stab the rum of the housing block. Now they blamed some guys we be with which made them take the situation more seriously. Mind you we are in a mental health program. Thus, prisoners with MMD's being trapped in a cell not getting yard etc. was the quickest way to set off a riot. One guy I know had ended up committing suicide and I just so happened to be at the door recording everything. It's a full scale riot not. Sirens, blood everywhere, halls flooded, officers in riot gear I mean we captured everything. Then I had that eureka moment - Ah Hah! I sent every clip to my man's Jt and he had merged the clips in with the other clips we had done. When we got the second version it was on point but my man's CEO Spazz had added his sauce on it for us and it had turned out to be a masterpiece. What a work of art huh? Yeah we did that and it was done literally in one prison cell. How amazing is that? We had quality music produced, a music video, we had messed up every music app you can name all we needed to do was create our social medias. One of my brother Armani Kelly aka Marley Whoophad just got out of prison. He had been on parole so he would be at home just trying to get his life in order. He was doing so great. He had found him a nice little job, had got him a girlfriend that he created a family with and he was the perfect person to help us. We would call building with the homie every day. He'd literally sit there with us doing research all day for us. We didn't have Wi-Fi connection due to these guys we thought was really rocking with us hating, so we would contact him when we didn't have the iPhone. He had helped us set our Instagram up, posted our photos the whole works. He had been an aspiring rapper to so we all supported one another.

    The last and final part to my plan was the marketing and promotion strategy. One thing I knew was the we had created such a great rap video that if placed in the right hands it would for sure go viral. I had sat back one night while my bunk mate was sleep. I was just listening to all our songs thinking. I remember asking myself had I ever heard about anyone who had been incarcerated making an actual structured music video I could only recall hearing about guys going live on Facebook or Instagram. I had heard about guys recording regular videos may be free styling or talking. But never had I ever heard about a real music video and that's when I knew that what we had was very unique. The content alone had been worthy of global recognition. I just remember smiling to myself saying, WE GOING TO MAKE HISTORY. WE'D BE THEFIRST TO EVER EXECUTE SOMETHING OF THISMAGNITUDE.I had formulated my next plan. It's funny because I still have j pays that I sent out way before I accomplished this, detailed my agenda about making this video go viral. There was one person I knew would be great for this part. My Mama believed in me so much that I could get her to do things of this nature. I told her send the video to every major new outlet that we could name. We emailed it to CNN, Fox News, Fox Local 2, The Governor of Michigan(Gretchen Withmer), we contacted our Detroit Free Press reporter. We made sure that it would be seen by everybody that would blast it to the world whether it be good or bad there is no such things as bad publicity (courtesy of Easy E and N.W.A. They never should've let me watch that movie huh?)I had also been building with my little home girl Elkendra (Super K) and she had put me hip to 'Crime In Da D', yeah I had her send it there as well and she followed up behind my mother with the media as well. Treezy mother also did the same thing media wise. She had even did the interview Fox 2News for us. You add all these amazing people in the mix with a mind like my own, we would conquer anything. My support team had helped us be successful. On the flip side, while all of these positive things was going on, there was another side of the story never told until now. When I first rode into Macomb I had been approached by several white corrections officers about the news article that had been published during the Pandemic. They had I formed me about the many staff assaults and basically was letting me know that, I wouldn't be conducting such activities under their watch. I had got word that one of my homies had been propositioned by a white female officer to take a hit out on me in exchange for a cellphone. Lucky me, being the caliber individual I am, word got back to me and out of respect for what I represent and the relationships I have, the individual came to me with the Intel. At first I was skeptical about the situation. I knew that guys would do anything to get such privileges. However, there was honor amongst thieves. Me and the individual had begun to build and he had informed me that the officers that were plotting against me and felt that I was responsible for several serious staff assaults and they planned to get my homie to give me some k2 laced with the deadly fentanyl drug. During this time the threat was real. It had been so much going on at that facility that I would have been a fool not to take the threat serious. I had only been there a few months and witnessed several overdoses and a handful of guys had been killed. This was hands down the most dangerous the MDOC had ever been out my entire bid. I knew that it was real when a guy had allegedly been killed over a cellphone. That was a wakeup call for me and it also prompted me to take such drastic measures and record those events shown in my video. But when my homie Sunny B had been brutally killed by another prisoner suffering from a severe mental illness, I had told myself that I couldn't play with my life. And the individual that had been found responsible for Sunny's demise had told the State Police that the rum who had an attempt made on his life had put him up to the task that only made things more realistic regards to the officers plot towards me. From that point I had devised a counter-strategy to thwart their plans. Me and the individual that they enlisted to do the job I had made an ally and we had started reaching out to family and friends to expose the corruption that had been taking place around us. It was so crazy that at one point I really feared for my life and refused to be a statistic.

Chapter 21 (The Aftermath). IN DIS CELL (MOST OF MY LIFE)

"Prison Made Huey Newton A Celebrity. Prison Made Eldridge Cleaver A Best Selling Author. Prison Is A Temporary Solution..."-J. Edgar Hoover On Fred Hampton No one would've been able to tell me that after all that we've managed to accomplish, that we'd be broke, abandoned, and almost regretting the entire situation. I remember watching the Matrix Reloaded and Morpheus had said, "I dreamed a dream, and now that dream has come for me." I had received the worse end of the stick. When things were up and we had been in position it was like we couldn't shake people. The media had a frenzy. We 'Broke The Internet' but even after all that we had been forgotten about just like that. I remember sitting up watching the recap on CNN and a couple other news media stations thinking, OKAYTHEY ABOUT TO RECAP THE YEARS HOTTESTVIRAL VIDEOS. WE GOTTA BE IN THE MIX. Think not. I would get upset to see that people were more interested in things that had no real value to the world. Everybody claimed that they had been for social justice and prison reform but I hadn't seen a trace of it. I was so optimistic about things. I remember watching TMZ seeing Kim Kardashian promoting her Hulu series "The Justice Project". I had seen her going into prisons in California and I had heard about her coming through Michigan or something like that. I just knew we'd be on her list. However, even after writing her a letter hoping to get her assistance, it had been literally impossible to reach her. I remember thinking how could someone say they are advocating for us but there's no way to reach them? Even after Breaking The Internet as she did, that wasn't great enough to reach such height's. Everybody I assumed would be in my life had walked away. The females that I had helped pay their bills, made sure they had the things they needed couldn't even hold a simple conversation with me. I would sense their irritation and think, DAMN THIS ISHOW I'M REPAID? Those that I had stuck my neck out there for and sacrificed for had burned me. Those that I had embraced as family finessed me out of thousands and I couldn't do anything about it. The business ventures we thought had been legitimately established had turned out to be a part of the scheme. Being that I had been hidden away in the maximum security prison I had no way of confirming these transactions. The people that we entrusted with our music etc had played us. Due to us being illiterate to the ways of the world we had been vulnerable to the greed of others. We would find out that despite having had hundreds of thousands of views we didn't have that following. Our fan base had been in limbo and when we figured it out guys had changed up the agreements and acted as if they had been responsible for our success when we did it with pure finesse. The finessers had been finessed ain't that something. Jealousy had consumed our peers and despite even excelling pass their achievements from a prison cell, guys refused to help us get any further than we had already gotten. I could barely get someone to respond back to a Jpay message, yet alone answer the phone for me. I would go to those who I had thought was down for us and they would try to charge me money to perform certain task after we had spent thousands with them. It was sad. I remember being in my single man cell talking to my brother Black Messiah and he would be like, "Gobe God. Make things manifest you can do it." I had more prisoners than anybody that believed in me but even some of my own brothers displayed treacherous tendencies. I was hated by the correction officers and envied by my peers. Being declared as a political prisoner had made matters worse. The governor had even been said to speak down on us for being what we thought was heroic. But I saw that the Republican party had made a field day out of the event. I knew that beside the creativity that we had exuded with the song and video, it was only broadcast as much as it was as a poke at the new Democratic Governor Gretchen With Mir for her win over Battle Ground Michigan. It was easy for me to discern that she had only been outspoken about us because we had stolen her shine. Instead of hearing about how Michigan's new Democratic Governor had been victorious over her Republican opponent, every time you seen news coverage out of Michigan my black behind was shown throwing up signs, rapping painful lyrics in one of Michigan Prison cells. I remember asking myself, what classifies an inmate as a political prisoner? I was only left with examples such as The Infamous Black Panther Party.

IN DIS CELL DEANGELO ANTHONY

Geronemo Pratt, Huey Newton, Angela Davis, Afifni Shakur, Matula Shakur, George Jackson and the other influential comrades of the era. Then I had found out that we had also made The Washington Post, and The New York Post. I would only see those Free Press referenced on CNN or its rival network, Fox News. Democratic/Republican=Political Prisoner!

It had become a game of chess. My life depended on being several moves ahead of my opponent. I had to prepare to withstand and counter both the administration and prisoners. I had begun to write attorneys on the civil matters that I would pursue as well as, criminally. I knew that they would not allow me to get away unsaved. They moved like any other political driven group. Retaliation is a must when made the fool. I had hired the civil attorney Ronnie Cromer out of Southfield, Michigan. This brother had shown himself to be so ineffective to the point it was like he had taken the retainer and never answered his phone again. My family and friends would be calling this guy on his cellular phone as well as, his assistant and tono avail could he be reached. Seeing that I was nearly at this alone, I had no sense of direction. One of my brothers rode into the facility and he had become my neighbor. He hadn't known what had taken place he had only been told in traffic what we had done. He had just so happened to be my neighbor. I had linked with him desperately, understanding that I could not allow myself to be just a viral moment. I wanted to be legendary and take back the narrative from my oppressors. After building and catching back up on things I had agreed to make him a partner. He had someone that he had vouched for that was willing to execute the logistics. I couldn't depend on nobody I thought I had on my team. I would be stalled out by guys when I would ask to get my content so I can establish my own YouTube channel. Or when I wanted my music to post on YouTube it had always boiled down to me having to come out some sort of finance. Everyone wanted a piece of the business. I mean everyone but what people hadn't realized was that despite not having what I needed out of my own assets, it took far more genius to do what we did. It took thousands to do what we did and we made sure we owned ourselves. Trusting people had become harder and harder. Everyone had their own hidden agendas. I was trying to further In Dis Cell which had become a huge brand, however people are so self-centered and ignorant to the point they almost always would abandon the concept for their own. Which is understandable. God Bless the child that has their own, but I had done this for all of us. We could've done anything with that device. We chose to sacrifice everything to gain it all. In the midst of all the madness of trying to dodge the administration, and reestablish my footing I had gotten bone chilling news. It was almost like some Illuminati-type stuff. I remember speaking with my brother Armani Kelly aka Marley Whoop and my brother B12 every day. Both these brothers had supported what I was doing and believed in me. As I mentioned before Marley had been the person that had helped us setup our social media platforms after my first page had been stolen by another individual that I entrusted. Haters was coming in all shapes and forms. Anyhow, I remember watching CNN and it had flashed 'three Detroit rappers missing after their show had been cancelled'. I'm not really thinking that it would been two of the brothers that I literally spoke with every day when I had the cellphone. Plus, rappers being killed or something happening to them was like normal in Detroit as well as, abroad. However, once I seen their faces on the news I had grabbed my mouth in awe. I remember having a conversation with Marley about ways we could take as short cuts to fame and fortune and I just was in denial. I'm like, THIS GUY DONE PULLED OUT THEMACHIAVELLI PLAYBOOK. He had been with me and Treezy every step of the way watching us speak our success into existence so I thought he had taken notes and done the same. However, that theory had been shattered when they had been identified amongst others as the missing rappers from Detroit. Real talk I wanted to cry because I felt so bad for them. Still oblivious to what took place, honestly don't wish to know, all I can say is they were some good brothers to me and I vowed to do this for them. It hurt to be able to say, a couple months prior to their deaths I was all over the news as the rapper that made a rap video in a cell and they had been known as the rappers that had been missing out Detroit found wrapped in trash bags. What a coincidence? I remember telling my mother about it after her asking me did I catch the news. I told her who Marley was. She had spoken with the brother countless times when he had helped us setup our corporation. She had sighed and said, "dang Deangelo, it's like everybody dying on you." I had begun to recount those whom I lost; Aunty Danielle Ray (T-Grymee Wife), Aunt Ernestine, Tyiela Autrey,

IN DIS CELL DEANGELO ANTHONY

Sharmane Brown-Dorcey, William "June Bug" Anthony, Kimberly Young, Javontae "Migo Money aka Young & Ruthless" Deberry, Grandmother Arizona Jenkins, Aunty Debbie Jenkins, Uncle Michael Jenkins, Uncle George Jenkins, My cousin Keith, Pucci Ciara mother, Armani" Marley Whoop" Kelly, Bad Guy B12... May they all Be In Peace. March 17, 2023 the day of my birthday I had ended up in segregation. I had been in a physical altercation with one of my guys from southwest after his disrespect towards my family. Prior that week I was building with my brother Jeremi who was on his way back to Ghana, Africa. I remember him just ministering to me every day of that week telling me to seek the guidance of the Lord. We would build about Jesus Christ and how he had changed my brother's life drastically. He had been through so much and I was just intrigued about his story. I remember thinking like MAN MY BROTHER HAS A POWERFULSTORY. HE GOT ME CONVINCED.

MAY BE I SHOULDSEEK JESUS HELP. I did! I had written some of the things that stood out to me from Bishop T.D. Jakes that I found helpful to me and I wanted to share them with you; "Passion Without Process Will Destroy You. "You Can't Be Fruitful if You Don't Trust Friends. "Don't Burn Bridges. "Resources Flow Thru Relationships. "You cannot have growth without disruption. "If you are afraid of disruption you are afraid to grow. "If you wanna know what your gifted at look at what people ask you for? "Giftedness without strategy is going to lead to injury" "It's arrogance that makes you override pressure. "I'm Open To Better" but they not willing to share. "God Sends help don't be ignorant and intimidated by other gifted people. "Back to the topic of decision. I had been in segregation for a fighting ticket. I had asked myself what is it that continues to cause me to self inflect? I hadn't even been able to get on the phone to speak with my family on my birthday, but I was on the yard fighting one of my close little brothers Sir Baby Tank-C because we both had two different ways of life that must be defended. Even after all the betrayal and backbiting I had been enduring for eleven years of being a part of the movement, I still fought for it. That had led me to reading the Bible. I had went back to read the Gospels. I wanted to see how Jesus had been betrayed and how he had reacted to his environment. I even went back to Genesis and read it to see certain aspects that I felt I needed to revisit. What I had come up with was that there was something greater than me, however, only thru man would this divine entity reveal himself to man. Thus, as my grandmother would tell me growing up, "you never know who you are talking to. You never know who the homeless man at the corner store is asking you for spare change is. God works in mysterious ways. "I had told myself I just have to trust the process. Show up and show out. My day would come because I had been preparing my whole life for it. During my segregation time I had been arraigned on the cellphone situation. Count 1: PRISONS -CELLPHONE VIOLATIONS which mean "did being a prisoner in a correctional facility, did possess or use a cellular telephone or otherwise wireless communication device in or on the grounds of a correctional facility without authorization..." The attorney I had hired hadn't even been able to be reached thus, I had been

IN DIS CELL DEANGELO ANTHONY

forced to deal with a public defender. I had been offered a year misdemeanor with 180 days' time served. But I refused to take the plea due to the discovery. The administration had not had enough evidence on me to convict me. Treezy on the other hand had been all through the discovery package due to his social media platforms. I had been lucky enough to not have had that yet established which had been what worked in my favor. I remember recently sitting in my level five cell contemplating suicide once again. I just felt defeated. I had seemed to never be satisfied and as my brother told me, he said that that's how I know I'm a child of God, because the devil is after me. He even told me about this one time we had got caught stealing at Myers and my mother had asked me why did I steal and he said, "I can't remember what I said, but I know what you said." I laughed then inquired, "what did I say?" My brother then said, "you said the devil told you to do it." I couldn't help but bear witness to the truth, and question may be there is something more spiritual taking place because so many things were coming at me from all angles. July 12, 2023 I had gotten great news that my codefendant G-Man had finally signed my affidavit exonerating me of the original crimes I had been accused of and all I could think was how blessed I would be to be released earlier than I assumed. Though the doors have yet to be opened I am optimistic and now working on bettering my life to return to society a more positive, productive and constructive man for society. NOTE: HENCE THIS MEMOIR, THE CASE HAS YET TO BE TRIED THUS STAY TUNED FOR PART:2 IN DISCELL (THE STORY OF MY LIFE) THE

IN DIS CELL DEANGELO ANTHONY

COMPLETEAUTOBIOGRAPHY. THANK YOU FORYOUR SUPPORT.PEACE!

EPILOGUE

IN DIS CELL "That a man can change himself, improve himself, control his environment, and master his own destiny is the conclusion of every mind who is wide-awake to the power of right thought in constructive action."-Larsen. I had been scheduled for Trial March 19, 2024 and was writ'ed out to the Macomb County Jail for court. Macomb County was like a vacation. I felt so good to get away from the prison. In an odd way I felt relieved and decided to take advantage of the situation instead of being a victim. After the prosecutor failed to finesse me into taking a plea for a one year misdemeanor and pay a fine, though this sounded so good I remember asking my attorney Marissa who had been filling in for my actual attorney Elisha. I had looked at this beautiful white woman and she smiled at me with these pretty white teeth. I then inquired, "this too good to be true. Why are they so eager to get me to take this plea?" I had then said, " their trying to sweep this situation under the rug and give me a slap on the wrist just to say they punished me for the event. "I remember this beautiful white woman say, "they haven't gotten away with nothing. Look what you did. You didn't let them get away. I hope you get out because you would be so great for society." I had reflected on the letter that I had written here and hand delivered myself. She told me the letter was so great that she is putting it in her favorite client file. I smiled and said, "let's go to trial. "When I stepped out the MDOC van I inhaled the air. It smelled different than being in some hick town like Ionia. I was greeted by the Sheriff deputies. They were so polite and respectful. Truth be told I am always treated with respect by the authorities. I learned to carry myself in a more mature, intelligent manner. I can speak their language. Once the belly chains had come off I had to step in to this machine. It was like I was entering an airport. I had never been in a full body scanning machine. That alone was like some futuristic technology. I had been patted down and then they recorded all my information. It's crazy because it was like I had started all over again. I was so close to the free world that when I stepped into the tanks with the other inmates I felt like I was going home. The harsh urine filled air intruded my nostrils. I looked around at guys spread out all over the holding cell. The guys were sleeping like baby's. The tanks were so cold that these poor guys had been tucked in their shirts like turtle shells. I made sure guys knew that I had entered the environment. Common courtesy learned off the prison yards. You always announced your presence when you entered shared space. I had stepped over guys getting a nice little spot on the cold slab. Things seemed to be going exactly how I saw it. I remember talking to one of the inmates. This Arab guy from Southwest Detroit. He had put me hip to all the things I was deprived of. It was so much going on in the world that it was like listening to some story. He told me about everything and encouraged me to get free and never go back. Then this elder guy had looked at me and asked where did he know me from? I laughed and told him how long I had been incarcerated he was shocked to find out that I had been locked up so long. He then said "I can't put a finger on it but I know you." I immediately asked had he ever been to prison. He had but not during my time. After revealing why I was down on a writ he then figured it out, "oh, you one of the guys that was on the news like a year ago? "I had begun to realize that I was more famous and known than I ever imagined. I had sheriff's coming to greet me. Everybody treated me like a Celebrity. All love. I had finally been dressed in and processed into the jails system. I was coached on how to activate my phone pin, store machine and jpay. I was amazed at how they jails provided more incentive for their prisoners. I had been housed in the segregation block due to my high profile status. Plus I was a maximum security prison in the MDOC.I had been on this rock that was directly by the control center. It was dark, cold and quiet. I had been in the last cell and soon as the door closed I just stood there looking around the cell. I read all the wall tagging and calendars written in pencil. I had immediately recognized that I was in the Red Zone. Everybody there was influenced by the Black Bottom. I then decided to make the mat after nearly an hour just standing in deep thought. I remember just passing out it was so cold. I woke up to a dep opening my food slot. They had fed me my first meal. I swear they fed their prisoners good. Their food wasn't bad and I was able to get extra servings. I had found out that I could get a tablet and it had educational content, the phone app and other things to occupy a person's mind. I couldn't access my account due to not knowing how to work the app. I ended up getting some assistance by the inmates that had been in seg. It's crazy because it was so quiet and you'd almost never know they were there. Especially being new to the environment. It was some pretty decent fellows locking there. I was allowed an hour out of cell movement.

  I couldn't wait to get out of that cell and call home. I immediately called everyone I thought was important. Need to know basis. After I ran out of the free collect calls with promises to add money on the phone. I then did what I was programmed to do. I started studying my surroundings. Learning everything conducive for me to stay the course. I observed vans of people getting booked into the county for whatever reason. Most cases were minor offenses. I see both men and women equally filling cells and being dumped back into the free world. I longed to be in their position. All I could think about was how long I been away. I admired fashion and was up close on women. I remember saying that I am about to meet as many people as possible to build a network so once I am back in the MDOC, I'd have things in motion.

  My first hour out the cell I almost learned everything there was to know about this entire jail. Laying on my back in another cell different location. I had reflected on how I was just in segregation. It's like every year my birthday comes around I'm in segregation. I had been pulled out of my Violence Prevention Program. I was doing so great. I was even actually taking the class serious. My teacher was so invested in teaching these skills to us. She even practiced them herself with her grandchildren. It was funny because she lived life dealing with the same exact thoughts and emotions just like us. It was crazy because we have been treated so inhumane at times that we didn't feel human. It's like we were different kind of being or something the way criminals were treated.

When I got to segregation the Correctional officers told me I had been in the hole for having an altered extension cord used to heat up my food, and to add insult to injury, there was a ink pen that they allegedly confiscated in my cell that had residue on it. WHAT?! Yeah I had been bamboozled. Come to find out the officers in 5 block felt that I had too much influence as well as, they claimed my name was coming up in nonsense. It's so easy to just put a ink pen in someone cell and say her was smoking. I didn't even try to fight it because I found that may be I was where I was supposed to be to make the right decisions.

I had been dealing with so many mixed feelings and thoughts about the two cellphone violations. I had been getting great news from my attorney with my 6.500 Motion for Relief and I didn't want to allow myself to jeopardize my freedom again. I had already tact on time to my sentence with the drug cases. I didn't want to see the parole board or nothing assuming my court proceedings in Oakland County would move alone as I envisioned. I envisioned myself coming back to be proceeding out of the MDOC with time served on my original case. I would head straight to the airport up out of Michigan.

Back to the present day at the county jail, I had dosed off. I had been awaken around 1am and was told that I had to move to another rock. I was so mad. I had been comfortable where I was at. I complied and was moved over to the next rock. This rock was totally opposite. There was mentally ill inmates that had been placed in segregation for disciplinary purposes. I had cringed when I heard the cell door lock behind me. I repeated the same motions I had described from the previous cell. Drained and just ready to get things over I went back sleep.

That following morning I had been reminded where I was at. This one kid was just going crazy. He was dressing the trustees out with urine. The deputies was so disenchanted with this guy that they just allowed him to do as he pleased. Taking his hour out, this guy had walked up the catwalk just fussing. He had looked like he was living in a cave. Hair all over the place. Shirt off. I was trying to use the tablet that I had and noticed this guy heading towards my cell. Due to the lack reception via Wi-Fi you had to hold the tablet out in the hall to get some bars then it would allow you to log in etc. I had immediately pulled my hand into the cells slot. This guy slammed it closed. I was so mad. I started selling him slum. I wasn't aware of the segregation games they played in the county jails. However, I learned very quick when the guy had spit in my face through the side of the door.

IN DIS CELL DEANGELO ANTHONY

Never had I ever been dressed out, spit on, or anything degrading as such. I wiped the spit from my face and went to the sink to wash my face. I understood the art of mental warfare. I had been around some of the best. I can't lie I had to get back. I must say that what I did to him made him run to the deps and tell on me. I was confused like THIS THE SAME GUY WHO WAS TERRORIZING THEM. He was now telling on me alleging that I had threw urine on him. The Deputies asked me what happened I'm like "aye that guys crazy."

I had been moved once again back to the rock I had been in previously. I was relived to get away from that rock. Come to find out they moved me to house the female prisoners due to over population. Oh was that an amazing experience. I had never been so close to women under such circumstances since juvenile. I couldn't wait to get my hour out to go see if I could pull a couple ladies.

The first group of females was something else. They was so aroused and wild that I had been flashed and asked to display my manhood to them. I had never been cut into like that. I wasn't interested in such because my time was limited. I wanted to meet a female that I could potential build a reap friendship with. I had remember writing them some words. Yeah, I found a way to communicate with them more discreetly. Couldn't front the place off. It was rare to have male and female inmates in the same vicinity yet alone talking to them.

IN DIS CELL DEANGELO ANTHONY

I was already being watched extra hard due to my status, but it was just a group a females all in the window trying to talk. We could barely hear one another.

I had been standing in the window watching them read my words. I had told them that I would love to see them flash me etc., but I'm not looking for any games. I was looking for somebody on their way home. Despite being so respectful they had started showing me their goods anyway. One of the Deputies had saw them and jumped over his desk to inform his coworkers. "It's like girls gone wild out there!" he said. I could hear him telling them what he had observed. They came out the bubble six deep instructing all the females to lock down and the females they had seen flashing they made pack up and moved them to another holding cell. THAT WAS FUN WHILE IT LASTED, I had told myself. I wasn't told to lock down so I continued my hour out. I went to the back door and yelled to check on the ladies. They was so mad at me. I was being cussed out. "F-YOU DEANGELO!" I heard one of the familiar voices say. I shook my head. I had told them do not show me their breast but they didn't listen. Funny thing they was also mad I didn't show them my package. It was crazy. Women had become so aggressive out there I wasn't ready for all that. That very next day I had been visited my attorney. She had told me that my codefendant Treezy was going to testify on my behalf. Also she discover a double jeopardy issue with being already punished for this even per the MDOC. I left that meeting feeling confident in my decision. I was ready to fight the case. When I had acquired the confidence I needed I had then understood that I had to take full advantage of this moment. I couldn't wait to expose them for their corruption. I contacted Fox2 and they had told my family that they received information about my trial and due to the national media coverage it was more than likely going to make the headlines igniting that flame back up. It had been almost two years since IN DIS CELL had captivated the masses. I had it all planned out. I told my support to be out there. Spread the news. I'm sure the people that was monitoring my communication over the jail phones saw exactly what I was working on. The very next day I was back on the prowl. This place was a revolving door. One minute they there the next minute there's an entirely different group. The females I was building with had been moved and the rock was cleared out for the weekenders. All the people who had caught cases but the judge allowed them a window to work or attend school or whatever. I had been on my hour out and as I was standing at the window checking out the line of females. There was this one female that was reading this book that had such an amazing title I instantly wanted to know here. It was like the universe put us together at that moment. This beautiful black woman had passed the window and I couldn't help but try to get her attention. At first she was just ignoring me. I'm at the window waving at her but she just didn't pay me any mind. After a few more attempts I had finally given up. I had seen the other woman and no one piqued my interest. I remember feeling that rejection. I was low key on low self after that. One of the guys on the rock with me who I had begun to build with had asked me what the females was on. He couldn't wait to get his hour out. He was the one who put me hip to being able to talk to the females being housed on this particular rock. I let him know what was what. He was such a team player he like, "bro don't trip we about to find something before you go back. "That night in my cell I had been watching a podcasting. The guy Step had come to the door and called me, "aye Alo! Real talk bro I think you should pull back up on ol' girl." He had been talking an out the female that rejected me. I had told him that I see that book and it made me want to get to know her. He had told me her name. I had told myself before I went to sleep that I would try again. The next day was March 16th, the day before my birthday. I couldn't wait to call home see how many of my family members wished me a happy birthday. I had talked to my moms and my cousin Joi. Something told me to go to the window after I ran out of calls. I went back to the door and there she was reading her book. She had her blanket over her shoulders deeply into the text. Finally I had gotten her attention. Displaying this beautiful smile at me warmed my spirit. "Damn, why you over there playing fake brazy?!" I had inquired. She acted as if she didn't know what I was talking about. I reminded her of how mean she was to me. She laughed and was a lot more bubbly than I imagined. I asked her the name of the book she showed me. "You got some chips?" she asked me. I was confused as heck. I was trying to pull her she was trying to finesse some more snacks for her weekend stay. "Man I ain't even been her long enough to grab store! I just came down for a writ from prison," I replied. All I was thinking about was getting to know her. After the small talk and realizing that we didn't have much time to build, I asked her can I get her information. She didn't hesitate to sign her number to me. I wrote it down and was so happy. She was leaving that following night of my birthday. I told her stay up so I can yell over to her rock. She was down for whatever at that point. This was very different for me. I hadn't had much experience close up with women. It's easy to game a female over the phone or jpay. Being up close just hit different. I had went back to my cell and I recorded her number on my important paperwork for safe keeping. After a while I began to think that maybe she gave me the wrong number. It was just too much like right. I get the female that I personally was driven to. Signs and symbols are for the conscious mind. Still slightly doubtful I called over to her reciting the first three digits to confirm. She had assured me that she gave me the right number.

 My birthday this year of 2024 had landed on a Sunday. I had turned 35. The day this female I had met was on her way home. I made sure I got that first hour out. 7am in the morning. I couldn't wait to see her and of course check to see if the number was right. I yelled over to her asking didn't the deputies let them out yet? They would be out first thing in the morning and would be out all day. They finally had let us out the cell. I was at the door waiting to see her walk out the door. She had been told that she was leaving. I watched as her short, thick beautiful self had walked pass the door. I almost had a heart attack. I was shooting my shot like I'm going to make this work. It was just funny how excited and happy I was to be away from the MDOC that the very simple things such as human interaction made me feel like I was free. She flirted back, just acknowledging that she see me. As I watched her walk away to freedom, I had looked forward to seeing her again. Crazy huh? I looked up and seen a familiar face. This face was almost like a sign that I wasn't out the door just yet. There was this Ex-Correctional officer that I was actually quiet cool with. He had immediately recognized me and was like "man I was just in seven block with you and your homeboy. In Dis Cell Huh? What officer brought that in? (he mentioned a name)"I smirked and said, "the warden!" I was just messing with him. After the small talk he had told me that control center said I had to be moved to a pod. I didn't want to go anywhere. I was comfortable once again they were uprooting me. It's like they wanted to keep me in motion so I don't have time to influence their facility. I was so mad. Only thing I was satisfied with was the fact I had made a new friend and that was enough for my birthday. I packed up my state issued property and paperwork and headed on up with the officers. I had been moved to a pod and placed on the eleventh floor. I knew they wanted to isolate me and keep me off the ground as if I was a cartel boss. I walked into this cell. Like all cells they were setup the same. I flopped on the mattress and broke down crying. I just was so overwhelmed with emotions. I had been cell after cell my whole life. I asked God like, MAN ARE YOU GOING TO STEP IN FOR ME? I THOUGHT WE HAD A BOND? Just questioning life and I noticed this Bible scripture on the wall that brought comfort to me. Pslam 23 to be exact. I had remember it almost by heart because it was one of my favorite, which is why it brought ease to me. That was my first sign that God was there for me no matter what. This cell was so cold and bright. I jumped to the top bunk to look out the window and what I seen immediately had me crying like a baby. Macomb County Juvenile Justice Center was directly across the from the jail. I saw the parking lot my mother had dragged me through to send me off. I began to have flashbacks of this place. I then wondered why would God play so many games with me? Here it was the place where all this criminal nonsense started at, became the place that also determined my freedom in the future. Ironic. I looked far in to the distance of the city. Looking at all the tall buildings and towers that's scattered the horizon. I marveled at how beautiful basically privileges are. In prison you don't see buildings. You don't see roads or urban structures. Nothing here to see but gates, and razor wire. Blue state vehicles patrol the perimeter. Gun towers overlooking the yards. I mentally traced my steps back through the old stumping ground's. I nearly imagined everything from 18 Mile to 9 Mile. I even saw where Meyer's used to be when my mother would take me and my siblings grocery shopping way out in the burbs. She would say that the food was better in the white communities. I admired the cars that passed my prevision. It was breath taking but once again so simple. The things we take for granted. I was able to get my hour out. I had dashed straight to the phone. My mother had figured out how to add money to my books. I called the number that the girl I met gave me. It was authentic. We had such a great conversation. It was so may things we built on that I never discovered in other female companions. Whether it was just a friendship or love on a more intimate level, we was just like spiritual connected. Henceforth, I am still in contact with this amazing woman and we just building a friendship. She been through something's and I wanted to help her through with what she was dealing with. This young lady had two beautiful black children. I love kids and I would listen to her being mom. She had been just getting over postpartum and still turning herself in every weekend. I felt so bad I had sent her some money on her books. Wow huh? But she had experienced a very painful lost. Her beautiful son had passed away for whatever reason and she was just destroyed. It happened out of nowhere. But one day I'll expound on this person and keep you posted on how things turned out for us. The day of court I was so anxious. I had been a little nervous because this was trial. I did my affirmations and was ready to face the music. When we got to the court house I had been pulled out ahead of all the other prisoners as if I was special or something. I didn't catch on to why this took place until after things played out. The sheriff that came and got me had been at all of my hearings so I didn't think it was anything in the game. He had told me the judge was ready and he wanted me to be ready. Okay. I was locked in another bathroom. This room was literally a caged bathroom! I didn't care all I wanted was to get things over with. I posted on the toilet with belly chains and cuffs waiting for them to come get me. After like 40 minutes my attorney had come to see me. She had told me that we have great news but there's also a catch to it. EMAIL: 76 IN DIS CELL (EPILOGUE).She told me how she knew the new prosecutor that had been assigned my caseload last minute. The first prosecutor used to be so mad at me because of wouldn't take her deals when she assumed it would've been in my favor. At least think it was. "They're going to dismiss both counts because there's evidence that was redacted from thee record that wasn't available for neither party. But they will push to dismiss without prejudice," My attorney explained. "Don't worry because they don't have access to the video because the video wasn't attached to the investigation package for the prosecution. "I had started thanking God. I was so baffled at what just took place. I couldn't believe that they didn't want to proceed with trial. However, the were aware of my defense. Mind you my codefendant was willing to testify that the device wasn't mine and he got it as a payment to place a hit on me. I thought about how they would be aware. I did blast them over jpay, via telephone etc. The MDOC Internal Affairs division even came to question me about what took place at Macomb. By the time the sheriff had come to get me I was smiling ear to ear. I just knew once I walked into the court room

Fox2 News would be there following up with the viral story they covered. I envisioned a packed court room as it normally would been every other time I came to a hearing. I had even invited a friend or two to be there for my support. However, that wasn't the case whatsoever. I entered the room and it was a ghost town. Only people was present was the prosecutor who had been in this friendly conversation with my attorney, and my attorney had been trying another attorney who sat in on the trial. I sat at the round table with an empty room behind me. I figured may be due to court not yet being in session like on the TV shows, people would be filling the room. I just knew the media would been in that group of spectators. The judge had finally entered the room and even to his amaze he was like "why is my court room so empty?" Edward Servitor was a popular guy. His family was a part of the Italian Mafia and they had infiltrated the legal system. Everybody in this man's family are judges. The judge introduced the case and it went on. The prosecutor said she had just been assigned this case last minute and didn't think it would be unethical to try me without access to the video footage that may have been exculpatory. The judge had agreed that it would be unethical but not prejudice to my rights. Because it was a new prosecutor that dismissed all charges without prejudice and warned me that they could bring it back up. The judge was so cool he kept it real and said "don't worry those video footage from the tazor only exist for like thirty days and the MDOC also didn't want to release this video footage because their officers were also in the wrong. I remember reflecting over what had just happened and it dawned on me that the reason the court room was empty because the prosecutor didn't want the media involved in the hearing. They wanted to do it quietly and fast. It was like a stiff. I just shook my head saying, LOCKED OFF IN DIS CELL GOT ME CRUSHING DOWN THESE BLUES/FEELING ALL THIS PAIN BARELY CAN TAKE OFF MY SHOES/WORKING ON MY HEART YOU CAN TELL THAT IT BEEN BRUISED/ I DONE GAVE MY LOVE AND LOYALTY AND BEEN MISUSED/IF YOU FOOL ME ONCE, NIGGA THATS SHAME ON YOU/AN IF IT HAPPEN TWICE THAN MAY BE YOUR SOMEONE FOOL/GOT TO LEARN YOUR LESSON LIKE YOU STILL IN SCHOOL/STEEL SHARPEN STEEL BETTER STAY AROUND THEM TOOLS/With that being said, I appreciate the support. Thank you for listening to my story and I pray that you found something that would help your life. I want to take this time also to say rest in peace to my brother Flock mother who recently passed away Aletha Latrice Webster 11-14-76 sunset on 2-3-24. Also I would like to commemorate my friend son AJ who had only been 4 months old before God called him home. God bless you.

IN DIS CELL (Most Of My Life) is a memoir based the life of DeAngelo Anthony aka Superbadd37, who recently, been most famously known as the Prisoner that recorded the rap video in a cell in the State Of

IN DIS CELL DEANGELO ANTHONY

Michigan, that "BROKE THE INTERNET". His YouTube video IN DIS CELL had been a huge media sensation/trend topic airing on CNN, NBC, FOX NEWS, FOXLOCAL 2 , HLN, CBS, ABC, GOOD MORNING AMERICA,METRO-DETROIT NEWS THE NEW YORK POST, THEWASHINGTON POST and THE DETROIT FREE PRESS etc., due to its graphic/explicit content displaying IN HUMANE TREATMENT of other inmates during a lockdown/riot at a prison in the MDOC. DeAngelo Anthony delves deep into his life story vividly reiterating his childhood growing up between Detroit, Michigan and Memphis, Tennessee. He reveals the story behind the scenes of the video and his experience being incarcerated since the early age of 14 years old through the Juvenile system ultimately into his adulthood serving a term of 20-40 years for Armed Robbery in the Michigan Department of Corrections. He also tells how he has battled mental health issues and other life challenges such as racism, religion and gang affiliation. DeAngelo Anthony works fulltime as an aspiring author, songwriter and rapper. Anthony writes music regularly and has hence self-published his previous book Million Dollar Nightmares under the pseudo Prince Angelo. His video In Dis Cell has been on numerous television shows, including The Real; The View; As well as him having hundreds of thousands of views on YouTube. He is currently housed in Maximum Security as a disciplinary sanction @ Ionia Correctional Facility, 1576 W. Bluewater Hwy, Ionia, MI48846. He can be found on

Instagram@InDisCell_SBV37@authordeangeloanthony@gmail.com

IN DIS CELL DEANGELO ANTHONY

IN DIS CELL DEANGELO ANTHONY

www.ingramcontent.com/pod-product-compliance
Lightning Source LLC
Chambersburg PA
CBHW052135070526
44585CB00017B/1841